Season 3

A Mac McKyer Sports Story

K. ARTHUR

Fulton Books, Inc.
Meadville, PA

Published by Fulton Books 2023

Cover By: Harbaugh Design, Seattle, Washington

ISBN 979-8-88505-545-1 (paperback)
ISBN 979-8-88982-197-7 (hardcover)
ISBN 979-8-88505-546-8 (digital)

Printed in the United States of America

When you lose, don't lose the lesson.

Remember that not getting what you want is
sometimes a wonderful stroke of luck.

From the wisdom of the Dalai Lama

CHAPTER 1

A Nonexistent Break

For a few days, life at Lincoln High settled into a comfortable routine. Winter snow and freezing rain had given way more often than not to warmer weather. The constant gray days and bare trees gradually changed to more sun and new green growth. Gardens were awash with color. The sounds of snow and leaf blowers shifted to lawn mowers.

The last two frenetic weeks of the basketball team's tournament run were over. Midterm exams and papers were finished with the usual mixed results for both students and teachers. And while it was true that Mack McKyer and the Lincoln Lions would have been glad to have extended their season another two games, they had beaten archrivals Jefferson and Washington to win the city title and swept through two rounds of the state tournament before being edged by Jackson High. (Yes, the same Jackson they had beaten back on their trip to the eastern part of the state in December).

The basketball season had been an intense three-plus months, a roller-coaster ride of both conflict and reconciliation. The team had won some games they should probably have lost and lost a few they should have won. But in the end, they had learned to persevere through both challenge and adversity.

For his part, Mack was tired. It had been a long full season. But it was a good tired. Thinking back over that time, Mack was proud of every member of the Lions basketball team, proud of what they had accomplished as players and more importantly as friends. And he was proud of his role as a catalyst in the hard-fought efforts to create team unity.

Back walking the hallowed halls of Lincoln High the day after the night before and the team's final loss of the season, Mack tried to pay some attention to each of his fellow students who wanted to say a word of congratulations or sympathy. Responses usually had to be brief. If he had stopped for a conversation every time there was an opportunity, he might have never made it to class. Sure, it was a good feeling to be celebrated, but he was indeed tired. Basketball season was over, and he was ready to move on.

And that meant baseball. For the six basketball players who also wanted to try out for the baseball team, given the extra couple of tournament weeks, the break between seasons was nonexistent. Cold and wet weather had prevented the other baseball team candidates from practicing outdoors, but at least they had been able to use the gym to work on general fitness and especially arm strength. Most had also taken advantage of the pitching/batting machines found at sports activity centers scattered around the city.

When the late arrivals—including Mack, Kerry "Red" Fergeson, Lamont Stevens and Carlisle Williamson from the varsity, Greg Jennings and Tyler Jones from the B Team—joined them, the hoopsters found about forty prospective baseball players, half of them freshmen. That first rainy Tuesday, everyone seemed to know to dress in sweats, grab glove and ball, pair up, and play catch. So Red and Mack dressed, grabbed glove and ball, paired up, and played catch in a crowded gym with twenty to twenty-five baseballs in the air at any given time. It felt a little risky, but after about fifteen minutes and no major head injuries, a whistle blew and they were all summoned to take a spot in the first five rows of bleacher seats.

That's when Mack got his first up front and personal experience of Lincoln High Head Baseball Coach Bud Hanson and Assistant Baseball Coach Coker Ramsey. In appearance, they were as opposite as any two men one could imagine. Hanson was tall, about six feet and four inches, dark, and—here, Mack searched for a word or words—sleek, svelte, and handsome gone to seed perhaps. Hanson was likely carrying a lot more weight around the middle than in his active playing days and looked like he hadn't shaved for the last three.

Boy, that's a bit on the judgmental side, Mack thought. Even with the extra pounds, Hanson still carried himself like the former athlete that he was. Rumor had it that he had played AAA ball and even had the proverbial cuppa in the bigs back in his day. It was difficult to see his eyes under the dark bill of the snarling Lion baseball cap. Ramsey wore the same cap, but there, the resemblance ended. He was short and stocky, waddled when he walked, and always seemed to be standing on his tiptoes looking for something but not finding it. Only when Hanson was talking did Ramsey appear to be interested in what was going on in the present space. And at the moment, Hanson was talking.

"Gentlemen, good news—in two parts as a matter of fact. First, the weather report for tomorrow is dry and sunny—all day long." There was a brief cheer, and a muttering conversation followed by a Hanson frown. "When I'm speaking," he said, "I don't expect to compete for airtime with my players. I'll ignore the interruption this once." He paused and glanced around the seated group. "So we will gather on diamond one at three twenty sharp tomorrow. That should give you time to get away from your last class, change clothes, grab gear, and be there on time. For every five minutes late, don't even ask—just run. No exceptions will be made. If you are late, you run an extra lap around the field—all the way around—which means on the warning tracks in the outfield and around the foul poles, side fences, back stop, and stands. Is that clear?" Again, he glanced around, appearing to pause momentarily with each player. *The coach's gaze was intimidating*, Mack thought, *which was stupid because so far, Hanson had said nothing but the obvious.*

"We've already lost about a week and a half of practice due to the weather. I don't want to waste more time waiting around for everyone to bless us with his presence. Right, Cokey?"

"Right, Coach."

"Tomorrow, we'll start with that run I promised you—two full laps, three or more if you're late—then I'll have your on field assignments ready. In case you don't know, we provide a selection of bats, batting helmets, and balls. Anything else you think you need is up to you. Now the second good news. Because of the weather, Coach Ramsey has gotten together about two hours of instructional videos that we'll be watching in the community room as soon as I release you. Much of the instruction material will be familiar to anyone who has played ball from Little League on up, BUT I expect you to pay close attention. You may learn something useful for the next few days and you will be held accountable for knowing all the content.

"Finally, we don't have a lot of time to get you ready for the first game on the schedule. That will be one week from Friday against Kennedy. It's not a league game, so it won't count in the standings. But I do hate to lose to those guys, so don't expect us to go easy on you. And don't expect that because you played this game and were an all-star somewhere." (Was it Mack's imagination that Hanson's eyes seem to linger on him for a moment?) "That you're going to get special treatment here. We'll be putting this team together based on what we know about you and what you show us in the next couple of days. The final team roster will be posted on the locker room white-board first thing Monday morning. Any further thoughts, Cokey?

"No, coach."

"All right then. Any questions from the peanut gallery? All right then. Get your asses in the conference room ASAP."

*****

Ever since the McKyers had moved to Columbia City from rural Iowa, Kerry Fergeson had been Mack's best bud. They had met late the previous summer when Kerry acted the friendly neighbor and helped them unload their U-Haul van. The two young men quickly discovered their mutual love for sports along with the fact that they would both be attending Lincoln High School as juniors. Red had made sure to let Mack know about early season football practices and they had both made the varsity team, Red as a second-unit wide receiver and Mack as the third-string quarterback. Through the ups and downs of the season, they had become friends on the field and off. Circumstances and his own natural ability had eventually thrust

Mack into the starting QB position. Team conflict had come close to undermining a successful season, but they had made it to the city championship game and nearly won.

Though there were many issues early on, particularly racial tensions, the basketball season had also ended on a relatively successful note. Both Kerry and Mack had begun the season as backup point guards. Eventually, Mack's talent level made it impossible to keep him out of the starting lineup and the increased challenge of working together with the team's returning senior all-star player. His leadership qualities became a vital part of the Lincoln team's evolvement from mediocrity to eventually winning a spot in the state tournament. Red and Mack had differed some in their approach to the racially divisive issues that nearly destroyed the team and it had strained their friendship for a while. Currently, they were back on speaking terms, and indeed, neither of them really wanted to risk their friendship by continuing to air their differences.

"That was quite the introduction" was Mack's first comment to Kerry as they made their way home after those two hours of instructional videos replete with Coach Ramsey commentary.

"Yeah. That's Bud and Cokey. What a pair. But you know, they do have quite the positive record for turning out winners. Seems like we're always in the top two or three teams in the city and usually ranked pretty high in the state too. Hanson knows his baseball at least as well as Phillips knows his basketball. We should do well this year too. Lots of guys back who played regularly, including yours truly, at second base. Hey, it seems like we should have talked more about baseball stuff, but we've had a fair bit going on with…with everything. I don't even know what position you're trying out for."

"Frankly, I don't know for sure."

"You don't know for sure." Whereupon Red dropped his jaw in profound amazement. "You gotta know something like that."

"All I can tell you is what I've done in the past—which has been to fill in wherever needed. I guess my favorite position is shortstop maybe because it's more in the center of the action. But I also like the outfield—center or left. It just can get a little boring out there if the other team isn't hitting the ball in the air. Oh, and also, I'd like to try my hand at pitching one of these days."

"I wondered if you were going to mention that. You sure had an arm when throwing a football."

"Maybe you and I could form quite the double-play combination if they give me a try at short. Anyway, I'd like to work out at several positions."

"Uh. Red light. Red light. You need to think that through, my friend. Coach likes players who know what they want, unless, of course, you're a freshman. And you are not that."

"But I don't know what I want. I don't see why that should be a problem if I'm open to trying to play where I'm needed. What I don't like is how rushed this all feels. How can they possibly make a sound decision of who makes the team in barely two full practice sessions? That doesn't seem fair."

"You're right, it's not. But remember, they do know most of these guys from at least last year and even the freshmen types if they played summer ball around here. They do their scouting."

"Fine for you to say. You started at second last season. I didn't see any Lincoln High scouts at the Storm Lake Cornhuskers games back where I played ball."

"Really," said Kerry, "that's what your team was called." He laughed. "The Cornhuskers? Really?"

"Hey, don't knock it if you've never seen us play, which you have not. We had some good ballplayers there in my day—Field of Dreams and all that. Besides, we were about as close to the Nebraska Cornhuskers as we were to the U of I Hawkeyes."

"See ya tomorrow. Good luck in the tryouts. You're an athlete, man. You'll be fine."

"Sure, wish I had your confidence right now."

That had been the prelude to the Thursday and Friday tryouts.

CHAPTER 2

Tryouts

The pitch came in much faster than he anticipated. And just as he swung, the ball dropped off the outer edge of the plate and he hit nothing but air.

"Not quite as big as a basketball, is it, McKyer?" piped up the batting practice catcher.

Mack did his best to ignore the trash talk and immediately got set for the next pitch—not any too soon. A high, inside fastball this time. Mack backed out of the box, briefly wondering if there was some message he was supposed to get.

"Good pitch, Jason," yelled the catcher. "Guess he doesn't like high strikes. Maybe you better try underhand."

Mack glanced back at the guy behind the plate. He wasn't sure. He thought maybe his name was Derek or something like that, thought about responding with an argument about what was a strike and what was a ball, and maybe—since this was only his second batting practice of the spring—thought about suggesting that the pitchers were supposed to be working on throwing the ball over the plate instead of outside sliders or brushback fastballs. It was, however, early in the season to let him get suckered into a back and forth that was unlikely to change the situation—*better to focus on just hitting the ball*. And he had to admit, so far, he'd not done that very well.

It was the second pleasant-enough, outdoor tryout day. The day before had been just okay—meaning that after a couple of runs around the field, general calisthenics, and stretching, everyone was given some opportunities to field the various infield and outfield positions. Mack was in good shape. Back-to-back basketball and football seasons had seen to that, but getting into a comfort level playing baseball had not come quickly. Even at his favorite position, shortstop, he had felt awkward and made a couple of obvious errors. In the outfield, he had badly misjudged one fly ball, breaking in only to let it sail over his head. Still, they had only been at things for a day, and it seemed to Mack that he was not the only one making errors.

Batting practice had been worse. Even the pitches he had connected with had been weak ground balls or pop fouls. Mack was determined to improve this second day and give the coaches at least some idea of what they could expect from him during the season to come. He glanced toward the third-base dugout where the coaches appeared to be following the action on the field. He stepped back into the batter's box, again ignoring the banter from behind him, and concentrated on the pitcher. On the next pitch, Mack swung about as hard as he could. Once more, expecting a straight fastball, the curve broke outside and he managed an awkward lunge resulting in a foul dribble down the first baseline.

"Can't hit it if ya can't see it," said the what's-his-name catcher, apropos of nothing. Mack had seen the ball just fine, seen it drop about three inches under where he was about to swing. Some baseball self-talk was in order, as in, *You idiot McKyer, you are trying to kill the ball. Just meet it. So he's throwing you curveballs the second day of batting practice. You can hit a curveball. You mostly need to focus, watch for the spin, and don't assume it's a fastball down the middle.*

The next three pitches were fastballs. The first two were obviously low and Mack let them go. The third was headed for the outside corner and Mack fouled it off. "One more, then lay one down," came the cry from one of the coaches. *Come on! Give me a chance!* Again came the high inside fastball and Mack's decision to let it go and wait for a better pitch to hit. The pitcher shook his head as if to say in effect, "What was wrong with that one?" The catcher's running commentary suggested that Mack was totally outclassed and might as well give up and wait for football season to start.

Mack stepped out of the box, took a couple of hard practice swings, stepped back in, and waited. The pitch started high inside again, but Mack was not fooled this time. When the curve broke across the heart of the plate, he swung evenly and this time sent the ball on a line toward deep left center field—at least a double in anyone's ballpark. He couldn't help it and glanced toward the coaches. They appeared to be in deep conversation. It seemed they had not noticed his one and only clean hit of the season thus far. *Ah well,* he thought, laid one down on a semi fastball through the heart of the plate, and ran to first.

*****

That Friday after the second day of baseball practice, Mack and Red again shared the fifteen-minute walk from the high school to their neighborhood.

"So what do you think of Hanson and Ramsey now?" asked Red.

"Kinda old school, maybe," said Mack with a definite question in his words. "Why do you ask?"

"Just wondered since you hadn't had to deal with them before."

"I'd never met Smitson or Phillips before either."

"Or Lester Symonds." Red smiled.

"No, I could hardly forget him. Still, you make it sound like Hanson and Ramsey are different."

"Yeah. They are. For one thing, and I guess this is a warning of sorts, they are never wrong—at least not in their own eyes. You know how Smitson and even Phillips would sometimes admit when they made a wrong call or maybe got unreasonably pissed off about somethin'. Not Hanson. Not Ramsey. Oh, they know their baseball all right. They know the game, but even the best of us make mistakes sometimes. Not them."

"Then we just won't make any mistakes," Mack quipped.

"Hey, I'm tryin' to be your friend here. Just don't cross them. They'll find a way to make you pay."

"Okay, okay—farthest thing from my mind. Though if you ask me, coaching is a strange business to get into if you aren't prepared for some mistakes, maybe especially baseball. What's that old saying I heard from my dad? 'Baseball is the sport where even highly successful players fail about two-thirds of the time.' And I sure felt that today, trying to figure out how to hit a curveball again after about nine months off."

"Phelps was throwin' curveballs? That SOB. He's not supposed to be doin' that—especially not in batting practice. No wonder you were struggling up there."

"You saw."

"I saw, though you did get good hold of one. You're not tellin' me that was a curveball too."

"Well, yeah, but I was ready for it that time."

"Hey, wanna play some catch over the weekend if the weather holds?"

"For sure, my arm needs the work even if the rest of me is tired. Maybe we could find a couple of others and go down to the park for a little infield practice."

"At 10:00 a.m.?"

"You're on. I'll give Ed and Tim a call."

CHAPTER 3

Team Selection

Mack's weekend seemed to drag on forever. Monday morning loomed like some kind of final judgment day, which in a sense it was for him. Though he tried to find ways to distract himself, his mind kept replaying the errors he had committed, the wild swings that had not connected, and the odd awkwardness he felt as his body very slowly adjusted to a different sport—another season. He knew that a few weeks into the season, he would be standing in readiness in whatever position he ended up playing, confident and relatively assured, ready for the challenge, looking forward to making the plays required, focused at the plate, knowing and expecting that he would hit the ball safely somewhere at least three out of ten times. He knew all that because baseball had been his summer life since he was eight years old.

Mack was quite aware that a lot of people, including other athletes and even his own family, did not feel the same way as he did about baseball. Basketball may have been the sport that came easiest for him, and he had (the record showed) developed into a very good football player. So why baseball? Why didn't he take a break, get on top of his studies, and enjoy a fuller social life? Why, indeed?

Simply put, he loved the game. There was just something about putting on his baseball spikes and trotting out onto a baseball field, even if it was only to shag fly balls for a while. Frequently, he would daydream about taking his assigned place—usually shortstop or center field, ready for literally anything—line drives, pop flies, and ground balls in the hole or up the middle, ready to make the play that would change the course of a game. Or he would imagine stepping into the batter's box with the bases full of teammates imploring him to get the hit that would tie the game or win it in extra innings, matching wits with the pitcher, coming through in the clutch on a 3–2 pitch.

Saturday and Sunday were restless nights. Deep down, in his heart of hearts, Mack couldn't imagine not making the team. But that wasn't totally up to him. And through the last year, he had learned more than once that Columbia City was not Iowa.

*****

Monday dawned, a gray overcast sky that threatened rain again. *No,* Mack thought, *not back to the gym on the first real team practice of the season.* But yes, he did know he was getting a bit ahead of himself. *First things first. Get to school early so I can check the promised posted team listing.*

Mack showered, dressed, scarfed down a bowl of Wheaties, Breakfast of Champions, and managed not to offend anyone except sister Jana with his sullenness. "What's up with you?" was about all she said. Not bothering with a retort, he raced past her on his way up the stairs, brushed his teeth, grabbed a sweatshirt, and made it halfway down the next block before anyone—including parents—would notice he was gone. This particular day, he did not want to include even Kerry's company. If possible, he wanted to get into the gym, get his glance at the team list, and head to class without anyone else being the wiser. The absurdity of his secretiveness was not lost on him. Obviously, everyone who wanted to would know whose names were on that list before the first bell rang. Nevertheless, it somehow felt important to him to make this viewing his own private event. Then he could go about his business with less worry about what everyone else was thinking—maybe.

Or so it seemed as he paused across the street from the main entrance to the gym. Mack waited for about thirty seconds, which felt like thirty minutes. Then seeing no one he knew headed into the gym, he pulled the sweatshirt hood over his head, strode nonchalantly toward the entrance, opened the door, and slipped inside. The light seemed dimmer than he was accustomed to. He rounded a corner in the hall and before he could duck out of sight, two of the freshman baseball candidates noticed him. They had obviously been standing in front of the team posting. They were talking to each other in excited tones; but rather abruptly, without saying a word to him, they headed on toward the main school building. He had his wish. He was alone.

With a deep breath, Mack approached the paper taped to the whiteboard. He looked quickly down the list. Then he looked again more carefully. The list did not change.

LINCOLN HIGH SCHOOL VARSITY BASEBALL TEAM

Infielders: Andy Chin, Terry Clayton, DeQuan
    Ellis, Kerry Fergeson, J. J. Jackson, Greg
    Jennings, Ryan Ostler, Carlisle Williamson
Outfielders: Jerry Corbett, Marcus Deshields,
    D. Ron Ludlow, Trey McCarthy, Bryce
    Quinlan, Lamont Stevens, Fred Waters
Pitchers: Louis Jones, Jake Levinsky, Garry
    Matthews, Jason Phelps, Trevor Samielson,
    Tyler Jones
Catchers: Amos Jenkins, Derek Mosier

"Congratulations to the above players. Please report to the equipment room as soon as possible this afternoon to be sized for uniforms. We will meet in the conference room after the sizing is completed. Sweats will be worn for today's workout. If you did not make this year's team, we hope you will support us with your attendance and voices at our home games. Freshmen and sophomores are encouraged to report to B Team tryouts, which, weather permitting, will continue on auxiliary field three with Coach Smitson. If there are those who wish to continue their baseball careers outside of the high school system, there are a number of community-based teams looking for players. Go Lions!"

There was more, but Mack had seen what he needed to see. He did glance briefly to the bottom of the notice. *Maybe this was someone's idea of a joke.* It was no joke. There, in case anyone missed who had created the list, were the large familiar signatures of coaches Hanson and Ramsey.

Suddenly aware that there would soon be others stopping by to view the roster, Mack made his way to a still-darkened corner of the locker room. For several minutes, he sat in numbed silence—the noise of shuffling feet, the muffled conversation, and the occasional whoop in the background. Vaguely, he heard the normal bell summoning all to their homerooms, but he was not ready for normal yet. Through a mental fog, he found his way to the tunnel leading to the football field.

He opened the gate at the end of the tunnel and walked out onto the turf. The gate automatically clicked shut behind him. With no regard for the fact that he was wearing regular school clothes, not sweats or athletic shoes, Mack started jogging around the track. Then he was not jogging but running, then running full out as though nothing mattered but finishing ahead of the twenty-three-person team that, in his mind, were all close behind reaching out clawed baseball gloved hands to drag him down. After one lap, he pulled up briefly, then quickly realized that one was not enough. Maybe one more time around the oval would help to stifle the tears that he felt so close to the surface. At the end of lap two, he dropped himself at the foot of one of the goalposts, leaned back, stared at the cloud-streaked sky, and prayed for rain.

Feelings are more complicated than we would like them to be. For sure, Mack was mad. And he was in a bit of shock. And as already noted, he felt like crying. There was also a part of him that wanted to laugh. The mad part was the easiest to understand. Expletive. Expletive. Expletive. *How could coaches in any sport make such uninformed decisions that so dramatically affect young lives? How could they possibly know, after two brief afternoons, whether anyone was a good enough ballplayer to contribute to a baseball team? These were very expe-*

rienced guys in their sport. Shouldn't they know how to assess a player's natural ability by now? For the first time in a long time, Mack felt like the new kid on the block again. Didn't Hanson know who he was? Damn it! Damn it! Damn it! He was…he was…he was an athlete. And not just an athlete. He was a baseball player!

Mack glanced around the still-empty stadium, remembering the struggles and triumphs of the football season. This is where less than six months ago, he had thrown his first touchdown pass, the first of many. For a moment, he again imagined the stadium filled with fans yelling his name—so noisy they could hardly hear the signal call for the next play. Now all that he could sense was a slight breeze moving through the grass and the rattle of the pulley on the field flagpole. It was a melancholy sound. Mack took a deep breath and then he did cry—not much. He felt embarrassed—even with no one else around to see his pain.

Two minutes later, laughter bubbled to the surface—not that anything was really funny. Maybe it was the shock still. *Was he on the edge of hysteria or something like it?* No. Rather, it was his rock-solid common sense surfacing—the part of him he secretly liked the most. Of course, the laughter was at himself. He had not made the baseball team. So what? He had not only made but been one of the key players on both the football and basketball teams. In a short seven-month period, he had made a place for himself in a two-thousand-student high school. He was respected. He had friends. He was passing all his classes. He had a date to the junior prom. Further, he had a relatively solid family foundation. And even more, he had been privileged to know courageous and caring kids who knew what real, actual suffering was about. How could he possibly feel so sorry for himself that he would cry over being cut from a baseball team?

Of course, all that was so much easier to say than it was to feel. Both the tears and the laughter remained close to the surface. Maybe they were not the opposites he always had thought they were. Regardless, he couldn't stay where he was all day. At some point, he would need to get up and face this new baseball-less world. But not yet.

CHAPTER 4

Then Came the Rain

For a while, time seemed to stand still. It felt like he had been sitting at the base of a football goalpost for hours. Time check? He had left his phone with backpack in the locker room. How long ago did that last bell ring? Did it really matter?

"Mack," he said out loud to no one in particular, "you never do anything crazy or radical. You never skip classes. When you say you're sick, you actually are sick. You don't drink. You don't smoke. You're not much of a party animal. You like girls, but you're kind of afraid of them too. You always follow the rules. Today will be an exception. And to start with, you can't stay here all day."

With that, he stood up and looked around the field, track and stadium once again. *First problem: How will I get out of here without going back through the locker room and gym? Can't be that difficult,* he thought. About then, Mack felt the first drops of the rain he had prayed for earlier. *Okay then.*

While the rain began to build in volume at first, Mack walked with some purpose toward the grandstand gates. There, he discovered the first two were locked. He didn't exactly panic, but he did begin to move a bit quicker. For a moment, he gave up on his escape plan and tried the tunnel gate where he had entered the field to find that it only opened from the inside. He paused again under one of the partial roofs overhanging the now-of-course-closed concession stands. With his newfound rebellious spirit, Mack briefly considered finding a way to break in to the concession supply area. Maybe he could spend awhile stuffing his face with old Payday or Hershey bars until the rain stopped. *Unlikely that and besides, I don't actually want to get into trouble for breaking and entering.* At that point, he still had some unclarified notion that he could have his moment of radical freedom without anyone knowing about it.

So far, Mack had avoided getting totally soaked, but it had begun to look like he didn't really have a choice about that. There appeared to be no way back out of the stadium short of climbing the ten-foot-high fence that surrounded the far end of the field. The rain was showing no sign of letting up. *No use waiting.* He jogged back across the field, choosing a corner where fence and grandstand abutted one another. Struggling out of his now-quite-wet sweatshirt, he scrunched it into a ball and heaved it over the fence. Then bracing himself against the edge of the stands and grasping the cold, wet metal fencing in both hands, he scrambled as best he could to the top corner of the fence post; threw one of his feet over to the other side; grasped the top rail; and slipped and fell the final six feet— letting himself collapse and roll through the thoroughly wet grass. Cautiously, he got back on his feet, did a quick self-exam, which did not show any permanent damage, grabbed his soggy sweatshirt, and walked swiftly away from his school. He imagined he now knew what it would be like to escape from prison.

Now what? Mack's first thought was to make his way home and at least change into some dry clothes. *But no!* What if his mom was still home? He knew she wasn't at work this morning. Maybe she would be out shopping or something. But what if she wasn't? And even if she was, what if one of the busybody neighbors spotted him? No, home was a bad idea.

Other end of the spectrum of radical ideas: What if he made his way to the interstate and hitchhiked somewhere—like Iowa? That would certainly classify as adventurous and crazy—too crazy.

Or maybe he could borrow some money somewhere and buy a bus ticket headed east? Would Randy and Susan lend him a few bucks or better yet, take some out of his next paycheck? Mack adjusted his direction slightly and headed in the general direction of the Sugar

Spoon, an occasional hangout for Lincoln high students and place of Mack's part-time employment. Another mile or so walking in the downpour and he was soaked all the way through. He could see the sign for the Spoon when he stopped short in the middle of one of the puddles he had learned to ignore, groaned outwardly and inwardly.

"You idiot," he said to himself, "the Spoon doesn't open until 3:00 p.m., and neither Susan nor Randal is likely to be there until early this afternoon." To make certain, he checked both front and back doors and glanced through the darkened windows. No extra lights. No action. No Randal or Susan James.

He turned away in search of another hope, found an open mini-mart, bought a candy bar, and used the washroom—mostly to dry off as much as possible. Glancing out the window of the mini-mart and down the street, hope emerged in the form of the old Grand Theater, a movie outlet that showed non-first run artsy films at cut-rate prices. Mack walked quickly through the storm to check out the marquee. He was in luck. A feature showing of *A Kind of Loving* was set to start at 10:10 a.m. He had wanted to see that when it first came out but hadn't been able to find someone to go with him. He paid his three bucks and disappeared into the dark.

Nearly three hours later, Mack emerged from the theater to a rapidly clearing sky. Though it was colder outside and he shivered a bit, at least the theater had been warm. And except for his rear end, he was completely dry for the first time since the football field. The movie had been well done but not exactly what Mack had expected. He kind of wished he had someone to talk to about it, but he could hardly have stood up and announced a post-film discussion group. There had been, by his count, no more than six others in the theater and three of them appeared to be sleeping.

Mack was standing across the street from the Grand trying to decide if it was worth it to run back by the Spoon yet when he noticed another male about his own age leaving the theater with what appeared to be an effort not to be noticed. Well, he could hardly ask him why he wasn't in school. As he turned the corner heading toward the Spoon, Mack glanced back over his shoulder. The other kid, if that was what he was, looked straight at him and—was that a half smile on his face? *Okay, that was odd. Maybe I should go back and say something to him.* But when he glanced again, the young man had disappeared.

The Spoon office light was on when Mack approached and he could see Randal moving about the space. Mack took another deep breath and knocked on the rear door.

"Mack," said Randal, "come on in. You look rather like a drowned cat or dog—if you prefer."

"Thanks, I probably do actually feel worse than I look if that's possible, not physically." He hastened to add, "I'm glad you're here. I came by earlier, but—"

"Yeah, one of us tries to get here a couple of hours before opening to catch up on the business side of things and make sure we're clean, stocked, and ready to go."

"I know," Mack said. And then he hesitated. For his part, Randal nodded while looking a little confused.

"Why don't you take a seat?" he said. Then he added, "To speak the obvious, it looks like something is on your mind. I hope you don't need to quit your job here. We've enjoyed having you around."

"No—just the opposite actually. You know how we had to schedule my hours around basketball practice and game times. I thought that would stay the same during the baseball season. But turns out, I've got my afternoons free. I didn't make the team. So I'd like to see about scheduling additional hours if possible."

"Hmm. I imagine we can work something out, but I can't help but ask if anything else is going on."

"What do ya mean?"

"Mack, I know I'm thirtysomething and kind of out of touch, but try to look at things from where I sit. Young man of my fairly close acquaintance comes in the back door of the eating establishment where we both work, looking half drowned. It's one thirty in the afternoon of a school day, but he's not in school. He is a decent student or he wouldn't be able to work here at all. He's also whatever passes for a superstar high school athlete—"

"I wouldn't exactly say sup——" got out of Mack's mouth before Randal interrupted him.

"A superstar athlete who asks for increased employment hours because he, quote, 'didn't make the baseball team.' Now what would you say?"

"All right. I don't think you're out of touch or stupid or anything. I just didn't want to bother you with my problems."

"No bother. I got big ears and"—he glanced at the clock on the wall—"about an hour before I have to worry about time."

"It's really not that big of a deal. Well, it is to me, but I mean not in the bigger scheme of things. I love playing baseball. I got cut. I'm angry and upset about it. I don't think it was fair. And I just wasn't ready to face things at school this morning, so I left. I ran away, got caught in the rain, and decided to go to a movie down the street. That's all. And before you say anything, I know I'm being stupid and I've probably only made things worse. And if you think that makes me irresponsible, then I don't blame you if you don't want me working here anymore."

Mack could feel himself getting rather choked up again, so he stopped and got up while saying, "It probably wasn't such a good idea dropping in on you like this. I'm sorry. I'll get out of the way of your work and head somewhere."

"Mack, please sit back down." Mack sat. "It is not my business to stand in judgment over you. Needless to say, you've had a bad day. Most of us don't get out of this life without having a few of those. But I'm not going to tell you it's okay. Grow up. Get over it. I'm glad you came by. I'm glad you told me some, if not all, of what's going on. We'll work out the extra-hours thing when you decide what your availability is. I've only got one thing I need to say that you may not appreciate. You need to call your parents, like right now. You may not have thought about this, but unless things have changed dramatically in the last couple of years, the school will have noticed that you were absent and called your folks. They are likely to be greatly concerned about where you are."

"Oh. Now you are going to think I'm stupid. You're right. I didn't think about that at all. My mom is probably hysterical."

"Slow down, Mack. Just call them. Now."

"I can't. I left my phone in a gym locker."

"Here. Use this one."

*****

Mack's parents were not happy with him, but they were also relieved to hear from him. When his mom said she expected him home within the hour, he didn't argue. Randy talked to him about a tentative spring work schedule but added that he "thought Mack should take a little time to think things through further before he committed to a lot of extra hours."

Mack guessed home could have been worse than it was. Not that there were a lot of choices at this point, but on the two-mile walk home, Mack decided that honesty was going to be the best policy going forward. In other words, he told his mom and dad most of the truth. He left out the part on scaling the fence at the football stadium and the title of the movie. He thought perhaps he was going to escape unscathed. After all, he was a "good" kid. But when he suggested that his mom could write a note saying he was home "sick," that idea was not well received. Instead, he was told that he was expected to report to the principal's office, be truthful, and take responsibility for his choices.

Well, crap! He didn't see how that was going to teach him any further lesson. Wasn't he already suffering enough? No baseball. Damn Bud Hanson! Damn Coker Ramsey! Damn, damn, quadruple damn. He went quietly to his bedroom and stayed there all evening. No phone. No connections with the outside world. *I wonder if everyone knows now. I wonder what they're saying about me.*

CHAPTER 5

Unnoticed and Unexcused

If Mack had continued that last thought pattern, he could have easily added, *If anything, I wonder what people are saying or thinking if anything.* On the Tuesday after the Monday of radical, maniacal behavior, it seemed to him that absolutely no one had noticed that he had been absent—much less that he hadn't made the baseball team. Hmm. Was this good news or bad news? On one hand, it could be that everyone was being extra sensitive to his feelings. On the other hand, maybe no one cared. Or perhaps those were not the only alternatives: could be that people actually hadn't noticed, could be that word had not actually gotten out yet, could be the baseball coaches had realized their mistake and added him to the team. But no—to that last one anyway. When he had gone back to the locker room to retrieve his stuff that morning, he had, of course, checked the list again. There had been no changes.

On the way to his homeroom, Mack had stopped by the principal's office where the receptionist had asked why he was there. And when he told her, she had told him to take a seat—that there was someone already with Principal Grandy. He would have to wait for a bit. *Geesh!* He hoped to get this part over with and back to normal—whatever normal turned out to be. The ticks on the wall clock in the waiting area seemed extra loud and the wait was long enough that he had begun to imagine all kinds of disciplinary possibilities when two surprising things happened at once.

The inner door to the principal's private office opened and out walked two familiar faces. The first was the principal who smiled at Mack, saying, "Hi, Mack. I'll be with you in a minute." The other face was one Mack knew but couldn't at first recall from where and when. The kid stopped briefly, nodded, and smiled a kind of I-know-who-you-are smile and suddenly, it came to Mack—the guy from across the street by the movie theater. And for the second time in as many days, they both were saying to themselves, "I wonder what he's doing here."

Then the principal was saying, "So I'll see you next week, John, and we'll set up a time with Ms. Walker." With that, the John guy left at the same time that the bell for first period sounded. Mack paused a moment—unsure of whether to stay or go—when Mr. Grandy turned, nodded toward the inner office, and said, "Don't worry, Mack. We'll take care of things, and Ms. Prentiss here will see that you have a note to get into your next class. Come in."

The rest, as Mack described later to Kerry, was relatively painless. He was now the proud owner of one unexcused absence. A second would involve a mandatory meeting with "you, your parents, and yours truly." Should a third time occur, "and I strongly recommend it not," disciplinary measures would be taken that he was quite sure an "athlete and exceptional student," such as Mack would find "undesirable" and that he certainly would not want such actions on his permanent record. Mack agreed that he "certainly would not." After the hard stuff, the principal morphed into Mr. Nice Guy and wished Mack well in his "athletic and academic endeavors."

Mack said, "Thank you," grabbed his excused note from Ms. Prentiss, and walked the now-empty halls to his language arts class. He thought briefly about how easy it would be to keep walking to the end of the hall, through the side door, and down the road toward whatever.

It was the whatever that stopped him. Instead, he turned right, took the main stairway to the second floor and room 244, opened the door, gave his note to the teacher, endured the curious looks of twenty-nine fellow students, and took his seat. He drew a deep breath. Life at Lincoln High would go on—*such melodrama.*

The meeting with the principal had allowed Mack to avoid Katy and the rest of his fellow homeroom students. He was not so fortunate during lunch. Hiding out in the locker room again had lost its appeal as had escaping somewhere outside where the rain continued to fall. *I might as well face it, and besides, I'm hungry.* A sketchy plan evolved in his mind.

Instead of jumping out of his seat in his third-period class and rushing to lunch, Mack futzed around with some papers, waiting until only he and the teacher were left. He then chose a very indirect route and loitered as much as seemed natural while walking down the hall toward the cafeteria. His intention was to join the end of the food line near kids he didn't know with the hope that he would not have to talk about what had been happening the last couple of days. He needn't have bothered. Mack's fantasy that when given a chance everyone he knew would gather around him pestering him with questions he really didn't want to answer was just that—a fantasy. Like his earlier walks between classes, reality was no one seemed to notice him at all. Everyone was sitting in their usual spots with their usual group of friends eating and talking. And there he was with a tray full of food and no place to park his sorry self, save maybe over in one of the corners by himself—and that would just be weird.

Again, there seemed very little choice. And there was Red waving at him from their customary table with a few of the other guys. At first, Mack pretended to scan the room without seeing him but that was ridiculous. Kerry was the only redhead standing in the middle of the dining room waving like a fool. Mack sighed and headed that direction, squeezing in between Red and James Dunahue.

"Watcha doin'?" Red asked. "Lookin' for Elana? She's over there with Laurie and Sharon Teigs." Mack had not been looking for Elana, but he glanced in her direction anyway. He wasn't going to be able to avoid that for long either. He waved. She waved. He sat. Then before he could get anything distracting out of his mouth, Red said, "So what's goin' on with you?"

Well, there it was—short and sweet, the question. What was going on with him? And right then, Mack decided that he had better work up some consistent answer to that. Otherwise, he would be in for enumerable conversations that he really didn't want to have—at least yet. Mack glanced at his food tray—the chicken à la king, the pea salad, the banana, and cookie—and a ready excuse came to him.

"Hey, give me a sec to eat my lunch. What's with you? Did ya ask Georgia out yet?"

Okay, then. That worked out about as well as it could, he thought. Red seldom needed a reason to talk and he did—right up to the bell sounding for afternoon classes. Mack learned more than he cared to—about Red's algebra class, the junior prom decorating committee, and the beautiful Georgia—to last for the rest of the day. What he later realized was that Red had not once mentioned baseball. Were they going to avoid that topic for the rest of the spring? Well, wasn't that what he wanted?

CHAPTER 6

So How Are Things?

No, of course, it wasn't what he wanted. But neither did he want to invite anyone's pity, which meant that he would probably need to avoid his parents as well as his friends for a while. And how likely was that? Another plan evolved.

Mack waited until the more relaxed environment of his afternoon chem lab to text Randal, "Am available every afternoon this week, including today if needed."

Five minutes later, Randal's reply came, "Good timing. Afternoon staff called in sick. Can you do a three-to-seven shift and/or all the way to close?"

Mack replied, "All the way to close."

Then followed a lengthy exchange with his mom. She was not happy that he was not going to be home for dinner and wanted to know what the principal had said and when she and "your dad can sit down with you and have a talk." What could he say to that? He temporized with "maybe tomorrow or the weekend." Then he did lie with the line, "I'm really not trying to avoid you." Which was, of course, exactly what he was doing.

Mack finally got home about 11:00 p.m.—tired (of course) and depressed. Fortunately—or so he told himself—the house was mostly dark and everyone (he initially thought) had gone to bed. However, on a quick trip to the kitchen for something to drink, there was his dad—sitting at the table, reading a book, and sipping at his own drink.

"Got a moment, Mack?" he said. *Did he?*

"Not really. I was just going to grab something to drink and go to bed. I'm really tired."

"I don't mean this to take long."

Mack sighed. "All right." *Oh geez, have they decided to put me on probation or something?*

"Look, son, I have some idea of what you are feeling." *Like crap, maybe*, he thought. "I know how important team sports—especially baseball—are in your life." This had been exactly what Mack was afraid of. Parental support and understanding were one thing, but right now, *they just couldn't help. He needed to work this through on his own somehow* or so it seemed.

"Please, Dad, not now. Can't we talk about this later?"

"Okay, but I will take that as a commitment. And last word for the night, I need you to think about something you may not have thought of—no response needed for the moment. I'd like you to think about joining the baseball team our store sponsors. I know it wouldn't be the same. We're not all young jocks like you, mostly guys just out to have some fun. But we could sure use you. Just think about it. They're all good guys, and I bet you'd have a good time. And it's baseball."

There were so many things wrong with this possibility, Mack couldn't find the words. He held up his hand to stop the conversation where it was and fled upstairs to his room. *Come on, Dad. Baseball for a third-rate commercial team made up of a bunch of washed ups and wannabes. No way!*

*****

It was late. He was tired. But sleep wouldn't come. Mack tried to quiet his mind, tried counting sheep—which magically turned into fuzzy baseballs—tried praying, and tried breathing deeply. And when none of those worked, he sat up, turned on the bedside lamp, found a pen and tablet, and tried planning his life—short term and long.

The long part was vague, unreal and therefore easier. He would get an athletic scholarship; go to college; get a degree in something not math; maybe be good enough to make it as a professional athlete for a few years before settling into a meaningful, well-paying career; find Ms. Right; get married; have 2.5 children; grow old gracefully; and along the way, do something to make the world a better place.

But for the short term, he (for several minutes, Mack searched for the right word and found it) felt stuck. *Was this just about baseball?* Even for him, this seemed hopelessly shallow. Nevertheless, honesty required him to admit that it was true—at least in part. Maybe there was more, but for the moment, he couldn't get beyond the simple fact that baseball had always been a significant part of his life. And now it wasn't.

If I had made the team, I likely would not be having this conversation with myself. I'd be getting ready for the season—looking forward to practicing every day, hanging out with the guys, putting on that Lincoln uniform, and representing my school again. Well, that wasn't going to happen! And I damn well better get used to it, he thought.

Okay then, what choices do I have? Besides feeling sorry for myself that is. And that's where the stuck part kept resurfacing. All he could really think about was that every single spring of his young life, he had played organized baseball and now he wasn't. He knew he should let baseball go and do something else—like try out for the all-school play or do volunteer work at the children's hospital or tutor disadvantaged kids or even take up another spring sport like track or tennis.

Sometime around 2:00 a.m., he drifted off to never-never land—another lost boy wandering Planet Earth, wondering what tomorrow would bring. The only sure thing is this: It would not include baseball. And that was a loss—pure and simple—which he could not yet see his way around.

*****

Morning came as it always does. *How could it only be Wednesday?* he thought. It seemed to Mack that at least a month had elapsed since his life had changed *forever. Two days, only two days. That's all. And two would become three and three, four, and so on. Until eventually, this week would be only a faint memory.*

Meanwhile, unless he wanted to opt for unexcused absence number two with the lovely thought of a meeting with his parents and the principal, school was in his immediate future, like now. Climb out of bed, shower, shave—a little bit if necessary—grab a bowl of cereal, brush teeth, and hopefully, get out of the house without having a parent-youth conversation. Done, almost. A brief pleading that he didn't have time for—whatever. He needed to get to school early to complete a project he was working on. "I'll text if I have any dinner plans," he said as he walked out the door.

Another slog down the street, along a slightly different route than Kerry and he usually took. He wasn't ready for company. He managed to time things so that he walked into homeroom and took his seat along the windowed wall behind Katy just as the bell rang. At that point, fortune deserted him. Mr. Fletcher poked his head in the door and said, "Good morning, I need to check in the head office for a couple of minutes. Personal study time and quiet conversations are allowed. Please keep the latter to a low roar."

And with that, of course, Katy turned in her seat and asked Mack's favorite question, "So how are things with you?"

"Is that all you potential psychology majors can think to ask?"

"No. How about how do you know I'm going to major in psychology?"

"Only a guess—probably because you are always so sensitive and empathetic."

"Yeah. Well, you always seem to know the way to a girl's heart and"—she held up her hand to forestall Mack's next spoken thought—"how to avoid a straightforward, sensitive, and empathetic question aimed at you. I ask, again, how are things?"

Big Mack sigh. "You really want to know?"

"Uh, yes or I wouldn't have asked."

"Just between you and me?" She nodded.

"Well then." And he leaned toward her to say quietly but firmly, "Shitty."

"Pretty strong word for you."

"Nothing else fits."

"Wanna talk about it?"

Another sigh. "Yes and no."

"Whacha doin' tonight?" *Maybe she doesn't know yet*, he thought.

"Not much. Afternoon's free too."

"I have drama club until five."

"Tad doesn't mind?"

"No, he's not the jealous type. We're cool."

"Same bat time, same bat channel?"

"The Spoon at seven, right?"

CHAPTER 7

A Katy Consultation

As Mack sat at a corner table waiting for Katy, he wondered again whether this had been such a great idea. So what if her boyfriend didn't care? The Spoon was such a public place and other people would talk if they were seen together, wouldn't they? And besides, what did he want to say about what he was going through? How would Katy understand when he couldn't totally understand himself? What could she possibly say that would make a difference? He was about to text her and call their meeting off when she walked in, waved hi to Susan, and headed over to Mack's table.

"Hey."

"Hey."

"Haven't we been here before?"

"I guess so. And I wasn't much help then, was I? No, don't answer that. I'm guessing this is a very different situation. But regardless, I'll try really hard not to give advice. You know when you said that bit about being a psychology major, I know I overreacted. Did I tell you? No, I know I didn't. I've been seeing a professional counselor to work on some things, ya know. And I guess I thought OMG it's showing. But you see, the good thing is I'm learning stuff about me and how I'm always needing to fix other people's problems instead of handling my own."

"You sound more nervous about this than I am. And I do know what you mean about handling my own stuff. And you were helpful with that b-ball team situation. You helped me see some things I was blind to—especially the racism. And I'm not sure the team would have survived as well as we did without you. And I never said thank-you. So thank you—a little late."

"Unnecessary. I didn't say yes to this because I was looking for affirmation. We haven't known each other all that long, but I've never seen you looking as troubled as you have the last couple of days. I know there's probably nothing I can do, but I can listen, okay?"

And with that, Mack decided to unburden himself. Whether it would do any good, he doubted. But Katy was still his friend. He had trusted her and she hadn't exactly fixed him, but she hadn't let him down either. What could it hurt? So he told her about baseball starting with "I don't expect you to understand this part" and how important playing the game had been in his life to this point. He talked about the high school baseball team turnouts and his feelings about the coaching. And especially he went through the events of Monday, his reaction to the posting, his choosing to skip school, what he had done with his free day, and finally, how depressed he had been feeling since.

For her part, as promised, Katy mostly listened.

"So that's been my week thus far. I guess it all sounds kind of stupid when I talk it out—even to myself. What's the big deal about not being able to play baseball? I bet that's what you're thinking—just another shallow, superficial jock who doesn't deal well with failure."

"Hold on a sec. Don't forget I'm dating one of those shallow, superficial jocks and he's not either." This was said with typical Katy humor.

"Okay, well then. Thanks again."

"You're welcome. So would you mind a couple of questions?"

"You mean a couple more?" he said with a smile. "Will they go down okay with ice cream?"

"Sure. You buyin'?"

"Yep. Gotta use up that employee discount."

Mack took Katy's order and thought about how much he enjoyed her company, even her efforts to be more psychologically sophisticated. *I'm not sure what she meant by not trying to fix me.*

Actually, I think I kind of wouldn't mind being fixed, if that were even possible. Back to his seat at the table.

"All right then, you've got questions. Fire away."

"Well, first one is probably irrelevant to the main conversation." Mack nodded. "How did you like the movie?"

"Uh, it was okay. I told you the title, right?" Katy nodded. "It was mostly focused on a kid coming of age back in the 1980s. He was trying to decide if he was gay or not. And I guess that was important to the plot, but I actually didn't really see any difference in the choices he had to make—I mean any differences than if he'd have been straight."

"Yeah," Katy responded, "I didn't tell you before, but I saw it too—a few months ago. I agree. He was just a kid growing up, learning self-acceptance—something we all need to learn. I thought it was well done. And second question: I'm curious. You don't have to answer any of this by the way. But I'm curious what your parents had to say."

"About the movie?"

"No, stupid, about your AWOL-ness."

"Oh, that's easy. After my mom flipped out when I finally called her about 2:00 p.m., she basically said how worried she had been when the school called. She insisted I get home ASAP. Meanwhile, she must have talked to my dad. When I did get home, she was very calm and then played the accountability card—you know the one that means they can't let me think I've gotten away with anything so I have consequences, etc."

"And what about your dad?"

"He was mostly cool about everything—backed my mom up, of course. Except he was waiting up for me when I got off work last night. He thinks it would be a great idea if I literally played ball for his sporting goods store baseball team. Of course, I told him he was crazy. I can't imagine why he thought I would want to do that."

"Why not?"

"That's at least your third question by the way."

"Oops."

"Anyway, are you kidding? Playing ball with a bunch of has-beens and wannabes. That would be stupid."

"I don't get it. Maybe you are just an arrogant jock. I thought you loved baseball."

"I do, I'm not, but I mean—" Katy leaned in toward him expectantly. Mack really had no words and he knew it. "You just don't understand." And even to him, that sounded more like a whine than a reason.

They both attended to their melting sundaes. Then after an awkward silence, both started to talk at the same time twice. They laughed at which time Katy swiped her finger over her lips as if to zip them shut.

"I was just about to say I'm sorry. I know you're trying to help. And I'm the one being the ass here."

"And I was going to say I don't really think you are an arrogant jock, though you sounded like it just now. I was only trying to get you to think before you discount an idea—even if it came from your father. I know a few guys who have played in that league. It's pretty competitive actually—maybe not quite up to 5A baseball but close."

"I thought you didn't know anything about baseball."

"I don't care a whole lot about sports, but I do care about my friends who do care about sports—including baseball, as boring as it is to watch."

"Boring—it is NOT." And with that, Mack took it upon himself to try and convince Katy the exciting intricacies of a baseball game. She went back to listening and nodding but did leave him with one last comment.

"You may not have convinced me that baseball isn't boring, but you have convinced me that you love the game. I'm just sayin' why not play it. Why do you need another letterman's decal on your jacket?"

What else could he say but "I'll think about it"?

CHAPTER 8

The Yellow Jackets: Live

What really was there to think about? Yes, his pride had been hurt. And no, he still didn't believe that he had been given a fair shot at making the Lincoln High team. And yes, again, he was still mad about it. And no, he saw absolutely nothing he could do about the situation—not at Lincoln High School anyway. But he hadn't suddenly gotten over his love of baseball. And Katy had given voice to what now seemed so obvious to him. If he loved the game, why not find a way to play it?

Reopening the subject with his dad had not been nearly as difficult as he had made it in his mind. "Sure, it wasn't too late" to start coming to the team practice of the CCSG (Columbia City Sporting Goods) Yellow Jackets. With all the rain and muddy field conditions this spring, they had only managed about one and a half afternoons on an actual ball diamond. They were scheduled to meet at the Lincoln Park Field (about three blocks west of the high school) on Monday and Thursday afternoons. Actual games would begin two weeks from Saturday, weather permitting. "Oh, and did I tell you, son? Maybe I should have told you sooner. I'm actually the team coach/manager." This may have not been the reassuring information his dad intended.

Nevertheless, with some trepidation, Mack made his way over to Lincoln Park that Thursday after school. If he didn't go out of his way, it was only a ten-minute walk, though that did mean skirting the edge of the high school fields. Without really thinking, Mack paused behind a small stand of trees near the left field line and watched the high school team practice for a few minutes. He didn't know the kid taking infield practice at short stop, but there was his buddy Kerry catching a throw at the second-base bag, pivoting sharply and whipping the ball to J. J. Jackson at first. A moment later, Lamont Stevens was chasing a long fly into right center field. And he wasn't sure but thought that it was probably Amos Jenkins behind the catcher's gear. Once again, Mack felt the sadness and anger sweep over him. *Damn it. I should be out there with the rest of them.* And with that thought another one, *Why am I half hiding behind these trees torturing myself? Let's get on with it.* He slipped away with no more backward glances.

The rest of the walk was pleasant enough. It was at least dry, even if the temperature had turned a bit cooler after the rain. Mack had packed an athletic bag with his glove, cleats, and a change of clothes, but he hadn't thought about where he would actually be able to change. *Guess I'll figure that out when I get there.*

The closest entrance to the park led to a winding path, which he followed about two hundred yards through a wooded area to the athletic fields. There was a large soccer or football field on the far opposite side from where he was standing, some tennis courts on the near side to his right, and immediately in front of him, three baseball fields. All looked lined and ready for play. The infield surfaces were freshly raked, the outfield grass freshly mowed. There was a chain-link fence surrounding each home plate and extending about halfway down each foul line. A few rows of bleachers were located behind the fences in both directions. Two of the diamonds were currently in use. It took Mack about thirty seconds to realize that the guy with the lemony yellow baseball shirt and similar-colored cap throwing batting practice on field B was his father.

"The wind up and the pitch," Mack said to himself. The batter swings and crack, there's a long drive into deep center field. That ball is long gone, out of here—a home run in anyone's league. But wait, the center fielder is really fast. He had actually run that baby down, turned, and let the ball fall into his outstretched glove—a casual, experienced gesture. Then he took a couple of strides and winged the ball on a line, one bounce into the third baseman's hands. Well, that was impressive. At which time, Mack's dad yelled, "Easy does it, Johnny. Don't throw your arm out before the season even starts."

Johnny? Hmm. It couldn't be, could it? Well, if they're all as good fielders as he was, maybe this won't be such a loser of an operation. Sheesh. *What if I can't even make this team either?* With that rather unbearable thought, Mack walked over to the nearby public restroom facility, changed into his sweats, and jogged to the dugout where he rummaged in his bag for his cleats and put them on. It seemed apparent that he had arrived late in the middle of batting practice. Maybe he could just make his way unnoticed to one of the infield positions when it came available.

"Mack," Dad/Coach yelled.

"Yes, Da—Coach."

"Take a couple of loops around the field to loosen up and then get with Josh when he finishes pasting the ball all over the place and warm up your arm. Then you can come take my place on the mound."

"But, Da—Coach, I'm not a pitcher."

"Maybe, maybe not. But you have as good a chance of throwing the ball over the plate as I do."

After Mack's run and warm-up, his dad called him out to the pitching mound and handed him a ball with a few further instructions.

"This is just to help everybody work some of the winter rust out. You are not supposed to strike anybody out. Throw it over the plate and let 'em hit. Okay?"

While Mack's initial response, "I'm not a pitcher," was partially true (i.e., he hadn't pitched in any actual game since Little League), he still had a reasonable idea of what was expected. What was almost entirely new was throwing from the pitching mound. (Generally speaking, mounds were not used in Little League Baseball where the distance from the pitching rubber to home plate was significantly shorter.)

Mack toed the rubber, went into a brief windup, and threw his first practice pitch about five feet over the catcher's head. He was anticipating some negative catcalls from the field after that, but all he heard was silence. About five pitches later, he found the range and motioned the next batter into the box. His first pitch was about three feet outside, and the next one almost plunked the batsman in the ribs. Mack stopped and took a deep breath. "Mack," he said to himself, "you are making this much harder than it is." He could see Dad/Coach out of the corner of his eye about ready to walk toward the mound.

Impatiently, he shook his head and waved his glove as if to say, "I've got this." And for the most part, he did. He practiced the primary instruction he remembered from times past, "When you throw the ball, keep an eye on the catcher's glove and let your natural hand-eye coordination do the rest." He wound up and threw the next pitch fastball right over the heart of the plate about knee high. The batter swung and fouled it off down the right field line. Mack was sure that nine out of the next ten pitches would have been called strikes. The batter fouled another pitch off, swung, and missed at another, then managed a couple of hits, a few sharp ground balls, and a fly out to right field.

Mack pitched to another three batters before Dad/Coach called someone else to the job. The only thing Mack ended up finding difficult was ignoring the temptation to throw harder or even mix in a curveball or two. The curve had been his best pitch in long-ago Little League days. He restrained himself and continued to hold the speed down and throw strikes.

Mack's dad called for another change, sending the man playing shortstop into bat and waving Mack out to that infield position where he stayed until another pitching change. That's when things got a little weird. The guy who had been holding down the center field position since Mack arrived was called in to pitch. Mack was told to grab a bat. He jogged in and was intent on trying to find one that was a good weight and balance for him. He had been paying very little attention to the new pitcher until he stepped up to the plate and realized, even as the first fastball sailed across the inside corner and the catcher yelled, "Steerike." Then he looked toward the mound and realized—even as the next pitch was crossing the outside corner for another "steerike"—that he was looking at the same John guy who had smiled at him in the principal's office on Tuesday and the same guy he had seen outside the theater playing hooky on Monday.

Mack stepped quickly out of the batter's box. The pitcher then spoke with a casual and rather-ironic-sounding voice, "Something the matter with those two pitches? I threw them especially easy for you." And he laughed. It wasn't a mean sounding laugh—more like the guy actually thought there was something funny about the situation. Mack, however, did not laugh. Whatever baseball would end up being over the next couple of months, currently, it was not laughing material to him.

He stepped back into the batter's box, took a short practice swing, and readied himself for the pitch. The pitcher rubbed up the ball, flipped his glove briefly, wound up, and threw. The ball came toward the inside part of the plate. *Looking good*, Mack thought as he swung with all the pent-up emotions of the last week, intent on driving the ball as far as humanly possible. Too late. He saw the telltale spin of a breaking pitch, lunged at the ball, and missed it by about a foot. His thought immediately returned to the similar scene at the high school tryouts. As the old Yankee catcher Yogi Berra used to say, "Déjà vu all over again." He looked back at the pitcher, who simply grinned. Mack did not grin back. *If that's the way you want to play it,* he thought, *we'll see.* And again, he took a practice swing and readied himself for whatever came next.

Evidently, some kind of point had been made and Mack saw nothing but medium-speed, straight pitches for the next couple of minutes. As he relaxed, his timing improved and he began to make solid contact, going with each pitch and driving the ball for several likely base hits—*as if anyone cared*. "One more, then lay it down," came the cry from coach/Dad. Then there it was again, a telltale flip of the pitcher's glove. And this time, Mack was ready. The ball again came in toward the inside corner but broke sharply toward the middle of the plate. Mack waited a split second longer than previously. He swung harder than usual, connected with the fat part of the bat, and with some satisfaction, saw the ball head into deep left field.

For a moment, he forgot the order to lay one down and began a home-run trot toward first. What he initially missed was the left fielder, off with the crack of the bat and running full speed toward the corner of the field. The fielder turned at the last possible second, reached up, and gloved the ball. Then hardly missing a beat, he turned and fired a one-hop peg to the second baseman. It was a fine running catch, and there were a number of appreciative yells, "Great catch, George," followed by several voices chanting. "Georgee! Georgee!" was what Mack heard as he returned to the plate, picked up his bat, and got set for a pitch he could bunt. It really shouldn't have bothered him, but it did. He would have liked to have heard, "Great hit, Mack. That's an extra base hit in any league," or something. Not just "Great catch, George."

As Mack waited for a ride home while his dad collected the equipment bag and talked briefly with the last players to leave, he sat in the dugout and tried some self-talk affirmation. He was getting a chance to play baseball. Wasn't that what he wanted? So what if it wasn't the high school league. And begrudgingly, he had to acknowledge there really were some decent players on the Yellow Jacket team. The center fielder/pitcher named John something, Gene or George, the left fielder, and a couple of the infielders seemed to know what they were doing too. *But crap, it just wasn't the same* and he was still mad about it.

On the way home, Mack's dad did almost all the talking. Mack figured his dad could tell something was bothering him and probably could guess what it was mostly about, but it wasn't his style to force Mack into baring his inmost thoughts if he chose not to. And certainly, he didn't want to hurt his dad's feelings by ragging on about how the Columbia City Yellow Jackets didn't exactly measure up. He wasn't even sure that was true. But if it wasn't, why wasn't John what's his name playing for Lincoln High? Why wasn't that left fielder shagging flies with the high school team? And still, the real question of the hour: Why wasn't Francis McKyer on that other field with all his friends?

CHAPTER 9

Are You Kidding Me?

The rain returned on Monday. Over the weekend, Mack had taken his dad's advice and sought out a recreation center with an optional speed-pitching machine. He cranked it up to eighty-five miles per hour and totally mistimed most of the pitches. Before his frustration got the better of him, he turned the machine down to seventy-five and started making solid contact. Eventually, he moved the dial back up to eighty and at least hit or fouled off more than he missed. *Surely, there wouldn't be anyone in this league likely to throw the ball any faster than that,* he thought. Mack guessed that the pitches he saw at Yellow Jacket practice were likely in the sixty-five-through-seventy-miles-per-hour category. *Well, maybe that John kid had thrown a few close to seventy-five.*

It was Sunday evening, a week after that first practice, and Mack could no longer avoid the long-avoided talk with his dad. He was sitting in the downstairs family rec room, watching a new comedy show he wasn't that interested in and so far didn't think was funny when he heard his dad's firm footsteps headed his way. *Quick, do I pretend that I'm really into this program or be honest and say I don't feel like talking?*

"Hey, Mack, what's up?"

"Just watchin' a new show."

"Any good?"

"Uh, not really. Have a seat and decide for yourself."

A few minutes and no improvement later.

"I see whacha mean. I think they need a new team of writers. Is there a ball game on somewhere?"

"There's always a ball game on somewhere." And Mack started flipping channels and checking the program guide.

"Can you hold off for a few minutes? I wanted to show you something." And with that, his dad got out a piece of paper and passed it over to Mack.

"I just finished printing off a copy of the team schedule, players contact info, and at least a couple of starting lineups and batting orders. Look it over and tell me what you think."

Mack put the TV on mute. His vision jumped immediately to the proposed batting order. He couldn't resist the temptation, stood up, and pretended to put a microphone to his mouth and read out the order like he was a major league home field announcer.

"First in the order and starting in center field, Johneeee Raymond. At second base and batting second, Larreee Chen. In right field and hitting in the third spot, Stan 'The Man' Borison. Playing shortstop and batting in the four hole, Francis 'Mack' McKyer. Seriously, Dad, me hitting cleanup. I've never had the power, plus I think your team will think you're playing favorites or something."

"There's nothing final about this, but you do want to play short, right? And I think your hitting will come around in time."

"Really, I can play about anywhere—well, except maybe catcher or pitcher."

"I don't know about the pitching. You looked fairly good in your stint on the hill last week."

"Sure, if you don't mind watching my medium-speed fastball sailing out of the yard several times a game."

"You may be overestimating the hitters in our league. Well, most teams probably have two or three guys that can hit the ball okay, but I'm guessing that's about it. You could hold your own if you decided to put in some extra practice."

"Moving right along, in the fifth spot and holding down the hot corner, Alannnn Alford. Sixth, the first baseman, Karl McKyer. You're playing first, Dad? I thought you'd catch or maybe play in the outfield."

"Maybe, if I had to. But we've got a good catcher, and all the outfielders, including you if you want, have better knees and speed than I do these days."

"Speaking of catcher, in the seven spot and behind the plate strapping on the tools of ignorance will be Samuel T. Jackson. Was that the guy catching BP last week?"

"Nope, that was one of our utility guys—Pepper Wexler. Sam wasn't at practice Thursday. He's the head coach at Jefferson and can't make most of the practices. But he works out with the high school team and can make all the Saturday games."

"Eighth in the order in left field: George Daniels."

"That's actually Geor-gee or Georgeena Daniels, Mack."

"What? You mean the left fielder that caught my batting practice drive last Thursday? He's a she—I mean a girl. We've got a girl playing left field? Holy schmoley!"

"Well, not exactly a girl. She's a twenty-three-year-old woman and not a bad ballplayer at all. She started for the USC women's softball team until she graduated a year ago. She is married to Josh Kelsey actually. He's one of our reserve infielders. Anyway, she told me she'd always wanted to play baseball, only after her Little League days, no one would give her a fair tryout."

"Geesh. I must be getting blind. I never even noticed. I guess she's a good-enough outfielder, but can she hit at all?" The last he added with some derisiveness.

"I've never actually seen her in a game. Probably she doesn't have a lot of power—either," he added, looking directly at Mack, "but she seems to make pretty solid contact."

"I don't know, Dad. I kind of think of baseball as a guy's game."

"Well, we'll see, won't we? Why don't you finish the lineup? I might add. I don't know if you know. We don't use a DH in our league, so the pitcher, whoever it is, gets to hit too."

"Right, so batting ninth." Mack glanced back at his dad's list with less manufactured enthusiasm this time. "Batting ninth and pitching: Peter 'Softstuff' Morgan."

"Okay then, I've listed the others too. Pitching is our weakest position. Softstuff pitches exactly like his name sounds. He throws about every breaking ball ever invented but nothing faster than a fifteen-year-old Babe Ruth league player. When he's got good control—I'm taking his word for this—he can still get the job done. But when he doesn't." His dad shrugged. "We don't have great backups. Plus he's over fifty."

"What?"

"He's over fifty, so sometimes, he gets a little tired."

"Great."

"Probably our first-line reliever would be Jason Denard, but he's almost as old as Softy. He's a little faster but doesn't have much of a breaking pitch that I've seen. And we do have other backup options. They're just not that super. Or if you want to consider the proverbial glass half full, you could say everyone on the team may get a chance to pitch before the season's over—maybe one or two of you younger guys. You did say you wanted to play the game for fun, right?"

"Yeah, well. No way am I gonna pitch," Mack repeated. "I'll be your shortstop or an extra outfielder if you need one. Can we be done now?"

"No. You'll see I've made you a copy of the roster with a bit of personal info attached so you can get to know your teammates a little bit. The schedule is on the back. Mack dutifully looked at the list of players. He tried to feel as enthusiastic as his dad obviously wanted him to be. There they were.

> Alan Alford: thirty-three, BM, service station owner, infield (3B).
> Stan Borison: forty-five, BM, owns a bakery, outfield (RF).
> Larry Chen: twenty-eight, AM, physician, infield (2B).
> Georgeena Daniels: twenty-three, WF, accountant at CSG, outfield (LF).
> Jason Denard: forty-seven, WM, pharmacist, pitcher, outfield.
> Sam Jackson: twenty-seven, BM, high school teacher/coach, catcher.

> Randal James: forty-four, WM, restaurant owner, IB and outfield.
> Josh Kelsey: twenty-five, WM, grad student / part-time sales at CSG (married to Geena), infield.
> Karl McKyer: forty-seven, WM, store manager at CSG, infield (IB).
> Francis McKyer: seventeen, WM, high school student, infield (SS) and outfield, P?
> Peter Morgan: fifty-one, WM, head of sales at CSG, pitcher.
> John Raymond: eighteen, WM, high school student, outfield (CF).
> Andrew Wexler: forty-two, WM, minister, infield.

"Whoa. Take the P? away from my name." Mack did another double take. "Wait a sec. Randal's on the team? My boss is playing on your baseball team. I didn't see him there last Thursday. I don't think that's gonna work—so to speak."

"I don't see why not. You know he's a good guy. And besides, I need someone to spell me at first. And he can hit a little bit."

"But, Dad—"

"But, Dad, what?"

"Geesas, never mind."

Mack turned the paper over and got the final shock of his Dad meeting.

First, there were the names of the opposing teams followed by the schedule of games. He read the team names over again with an attempt at a nonjudgmental shake of his head and an internal roll of the eyes. There they were: The Swedish Meatballs, The Callapa Bay Oysters, The First Responders, Charlie's Angels, The Old Deli Grand Salamis, The Black Knights, and of course, The Columbia Sporting Goods Yellow Jackets.

"Seriously, Dad, Charlie's Angels."

"Hey, that's the team from the First Congregational Church. Their minister's first name is Charlie."

"Of course, it is."

Mack glanced further down the page. And then he did an even more pronounced double take.

"Is this for real?" His dad nodded.

"Are you serious?"

"You keep asking that, of course."

"I can't believe you didn't tell me before now."

"Would it have made any difference?"

Mack didn't answer right away. He kept returning to the game schedule and the last weekend of the season. The games started the first part of May and continued with two each week through June. Then there was a brief holiday break over the Fourth of July, another week of regular schedule followed by the dates July 16 through 18, and then a final notification: "The league winner will then play a best two of three series with the Lincoln High School boy's baseball team."

CHAPTER 10

In the Swing

Mack tried to remain cool about his new baseball commitment, telling himself that he could back out anytime. He even settled on the reasonably good excuse he would claim when asked why he had quit the team. "I really wanted to play ball," he would say, "but just found that I was too busy with schoolwork and a regular job. Maybe next year." Yeah, his dad would be a little disappointed, but he'd get over it.

That, however, was before he got into the swing of actually playing ball. Those couple of weeks before the Yellow Jacket's first game flew by. And yes, Mack's life was busy. He was now working three four-hour shifts a week at the Spoon. Teachers were still piling on the homework. Even with a limited social life, he could easily have made good use of that full-plate excuse. Yet when Tuesday, Thursday, and Saturday afternoons rolled around, Mack felt an extra spring in his step. Admitting it might have been hard at first but there was no doubt he was looking forward to Yellow Jacket baseball practice. All of it—regular infield workouts, including the focus on real-game situations. "Okay, guys. Runners on first and second—one out—know what you're going to do before the ball is hit." Chasing fly balls in the outfield, making the throws to the bases or to the right cut-off person, and hitting—pepper games to work on basic hand-eye coordination, bat control and bunting, and of course, taking a turn against live pitching.

The weather certainly helped. Spring had appeared in earnest—budding trees, flowers, the warmth of the sun, the eternal hope of new life. Yes, there were challenges to face in his world. He hadn't made his high school baseball team, but he was young, he was coordinated and strong, he was a talented athlete (no matter what some high school coaches might think), and he was ready to take on the Grand Salamis or Charlie's Angels or whomever.

School was a slightly different deal. Mack had gotten use to a certain amount of—*what would the right word be?—notoriety maybe.* He had nearly forgotten how slow his reputation as a star athlete had taken to develop the previous fall. While he was still the third-string quarterback, no one seemed to know or care that he was even on the football team. And sometimes it seemed like no one cared what he thought—period. Then within something like two weeks, he had become a starter—first as the team kicker. Then when a key injury and academic ineligibility sidelined both of the guys above him on the team pecking order, he became the first-team quarterback.

Quite suddenly, people cared what he thought. Kids who had passed by in the school hallways without a nod or had ignored him in class began to greet him by name, asked how he and/or the team was doing, and even wanted his opinion about other players, national sports figures, teachers, new movies, and whether he liked a certain girl. This wave of notoriety or popularity (*if that word is preferred*) continued when he made and then became a central figure on the basketball team.

Maybe it was—in fact, he was almost certain it was—his imagination that as March blossomed into April, his fellow students were now less interested in him or what he had to say. *The reality is probably more that my ego has taken a major hit,* he thought. *Or maybe I gave up too easily. I could have begged the coaches for another shot. I could have bitten my pride, asked to join the junior varsity, and worked my way back up. Or if varsity sports are so important to me, I could have gone out for track. I can jump pretty high and run kind of fast. And hey, my tennis game isn't bad. I could practice hard, and well, the best athletes don't even play tennis. Maybe I could play enough matches to earn a letter.*

Or I could just grow up. Like Katy always says, 'What's the big deal about playing sports anyway? Does it make you a better person? There were other things to get excited about, right?' There's always the all-school play. Who wouldn't want to pretend to be someone else for a couple of months? Or how about, as Mom is always saying, finding a way to use my full brain, put in more study hours, and actually make the honor roll for once? Commit to regular volunteer work at the hospital?

Then, of course, there's Elana. Probably it's not a bad guess that she would like more of my time. Not that I've actually been avoiding or ignoring her, but she is kind of sensitive that way. Maybe if we set a time to go out every week or twice a week even—once to just hang out for a couple of hours and once to go on an actual date. She'd probably like that. Would I like that? Do I even want to have—you know, like—a regular girlfriend?

And also, there're my guy friends. Getting down to the community center and playing some round ball with Nate and the guys would be cool. Hanging out more with Kerry, Lamont, Tad, Jeremy, Jason, etc. Maybe having a bunch of guys over for a game night. But that's kind of where I started. Lots of my friends will want to talk baseball, especially Red and the other guys who did make the team. I'd probably make them feel uncomfortable. I'd feel uncomfortable. Crap—just crap. It wasn't supposed to be this way! Enough already! Enough moaning. Enough feeling sorry for yourself. Let's just play ball! To hell with the Lions. Let's go, Yellow Jackets.

So back and forth went his mind—obsessing for a while about what might have been, allowing a bit of depression to sink in again. But then as the days got a little brighter and longer, Mack rediscovered his love of baseball. No, it wasn't what he had planned. Yes, it was just a small-time commercial league. Still, the more he saw the ball—in the field and at the plate—the more connected he felt not only to baseball but to the rest of his life.

Mack mused, *I know it's stupid. It's only a game, it's not even a second-team high school league, my dad's the coach, there's a girl on the team for god's sake and two guys almost old enough to be my grandfathers, we play teams named Charlie's Angels and the Grand Salamis, and it'll mean very little in the overall scheme of things. But it's fun. And I'm having fun. At least for now, I'm in the swing of it all—so to speak.*

With that, it was three thirty Tuesday afternoon, then Thursday, then Saturday. And soon, his turn to step into the batter's box and take his swings again.

CHAPTER 11

First Game

The Saturday morning of the first game on the Yellow Jackets schedule dawned a little on the cool side, but it was clear. There wasn't a single cloud in the sky. It might be a bit chilly for any spectators, but as far as Mack was concerned, it was close to perfect. The game against the First Responders was to start at 4:00 p.m. It was a half hour before game time and the Yellow Jackets—in their bright, new, yellow-and-black-striped uniform tops—were warming up along the left field foul line when their opposition arrived ON A FIRETRUCK with brief siren spurts accompanying them. The guys that emerged from the truck were dressed in red-and-blue uniforms and all seemed to fit the muscular, athletic stereotype of their profession. It was hard to tell if their arrival was supposed to be intimidating or just part of the fun. Mack couldn't help but wonder if they played the game as good as they looked. If so, it might be a challenging afternoon for the YJs.

As soon as the early afternoon game between the Grand Salamis (a deli) and the Swedish Meatballs (not a deli but oddly enough, a hospital) was over, the Jackets took the field for a brief batting practice (three swings each) and infield. While the First Responders were taking their turn, coach/Dad called the team together. *I guess I need to get rid of the coach/Dad and get used to referring to him as either coach or Karl,* he thought. *Could I really consider calling my dad by his first name?*

The team sat in a circle in the shade of a large oak tree well back from the left field line. Coach/Dad got their attention.

"Make yourselves comfortable. We've got a few minutes." *Oh geez, I hope he's not about to give us some kind of rah-rah pep talk.* "We're the home team today, so we'll start out in the field. I really only have one—well, two, well, three—things to say besides announcing the starting lineup. First, have fun out there. That's what it's all about. Second, everyone who wants to will get a chance to play, so don't worry if you're not starting. We'll get you in. And third, remember the umpires are not exactly professional at this level, so give them a break. If they miss a call, they miss a call. No use getting your knickers in a twist." *Knickers in a twist, Dad? Let it go.*

"Okay then, Johnny, you'll start in center and bat first. Larry, you're at second and batting second. Stan, right field and third in the order. Sam, you're our catcher and cleanup guy. Alan, at the hot corner and batting in the five hole. Randal, you're on first and batting sixth. Georgeena, you'll start in left and bat seventh. Mack, you'll be at short and in the eighth slot." *Well, I did tell him I didn't want to bat cleanup, but eighth? I think I've been better than that in practice*, he thought. "Finally, last but not least, Peter, you'll start on the mound. Any questions?" He glanced around the circle.

"Yeah, Karl."

"Yes, Jason."

"Not that I think he will, but if Softy falters in the early innings, who do you have in mind for relief? And where do we warm up?"

"I'm figuring on Peter for at least five solid innings, but if we need to make a change sooner, we will. I'd like you and Andy to warm up your arms starting in the fifth unless I say so before that. You'll have to throw down here outside the fence line. And I know there's no real bullpen or mound. That's a problem. You'll just have to adjust when you get in the game. Besides these two, some of you guys who are starting in the field may have to warm up your pitching arms while our team is batting. And unless," he said with an attempt at humor, "we have some late-season call-ups, this is how we'll roll for the summer. Okay, I see that the umps have arrived. Let's get to it."

Mack jogged out to his shortstop position and along with the other infielders, took routine thrown grounders from Randal James at first base. It wasn't the same as a sharply hit ground ball off a bat, but at least they could keep their arms ready when those chances did come. That, of course, was one of the major challenges of baseball. It was always possible that a person could play an entire nine-inning game and not have a single chance to catch a ball and/or throw someone out. The point was to always be ready, always, and know what you will do if and when the ball does come at you.

About three minutes and ten throws to first later, the umpire called, "Play ball." Peter "Softstuff" Morgan threw his final warm-up pitch. Sam Jackson threw the ball to Larry Chen at the second-base bag. Larry tossed the ball to Mack and Mack to Alan Alford at third. Alan walked the ball over to Softstuff, trotted back to his position, and the first game of the season was finally underway.

True to his nickname, Peter Morgan did not throw the ball very hard. But he did throw strikes and often with a small or large break that messed with the batter's timing. And as long as he kept his pitches down, most batters hit the ball on the ground. This was a good thing for keeping the infielders directly involved in the game. The First Responder leadoff hitter ground the ball sharply but directly at Alan Alford at third. Alan played the ball cleanly on two hops and made the easy throw to Randal James at first. A good start. The next Responder dribbled a grounder weakly to Larry Chen, who charged, gloved the ball, and snapped a quick underhand toss to Randal for the second out. The third batter in the order did not hit the ball particularly hard but in the right place. Mack gloved it deep in the shortstop third-base hole, but his throw was too high and too late and sailed well over Randal's outstretched glove. Even with the catcher attempting to back up the play, the runner scooted quickly to second base.

Dang, an error on my very first play of the season. I shouldn't have thrown it. He had already beaten it out. And now I've put him in scoring position.

Mack's error didn't make any difference when on a 2–2 count, Morgan made the mistake of leaving a soft curve up in the strike zone. The cleanup hitter did not miss it. His long fly ball sailed well out of reach beyond the left field fence. A strikeout ended the first half inning, but the Responders led 2–0.

The usual chatter greeted Mack as he took a spot in the dugout between Alford and Kelsey. No one mentioned his error. They were all focused on John Raymond as he picked out a couple of bats to swing and strode to the plate: "Come on now, Johnny. Everybody hits," "Our turn now. Let's get 'em back," and "You're the man, John. Get us started now." And from somewhere on the bleachers on the opposite side of the field, there was a singsong chant in a fake, high, female voice, saying, "Johnny Rainbow. Johnny Rainbow. Johnny Rainbow."

John Raymond had stepped up to the plate, but when the chant began, he quickly stepped out and glared in the direction of the voices. The umpire initially lifted up his hand for a time-out but then waved John back to the plate and added, rather forcefully, "Play ball!" The chant continued. John again glanced in their direction, then tapped his bat on the plate and tried to bring his attention back to the pitcher. He swung hard at the first two pitches, then ground weakly back to the mound.

Meanwhile, Mack looked up and down the bench. Most of his teammates were gazing toward the field or the First Responder dugout. Occasionally, someone would yell encouragement to the batter.

Mack nudged Josh Kelsey and quietly asked, "What's the deal with the Johnny Rainbow stuff? I don't get it."

"You asked the wrong guy, Mack. I don't know for sure. And what I know isn't mine to share."

"Well, that just makes me more curious. I promise I won't say a word about where I got my material when I go on stage next week."

"Listen, as far as I'm concerned, it's just not funny. If you really want to know, talk to Johnny after the game or at practice next week."

He said the last as Raymond was walking back to take a place at the end of the bench. Mack glanced his direction, and when their eyes met, he mouthed the question, "Are you okay?" without knowing what he was asking about. John smiled, rolled his eyes a bit, and nodded.

The Jackets went down in order in the first as Alford struck out and Borison lifted a high pop fly to center. Mack grabbed his glove, and John joined him as they jogged out to their defensive positions.

Before he headed to center field, John managed to ask, "Catch you later?"

And Mack responded, "Sure, after the game."

The next couple of hours were almost totally about baseball. For the first five innings, the Yellow Jackets struggled offensively, except for two scattered singles: one a Georgeena Daniels single to right center in the third and the other a Sam Jackson line drive up the middle in the fourth. No one was making solid contact with the baseball. Neither runner advanced. Meanwhile, the First Responders continued to score nearly every inning and led 7–0 going into the bottom of the sixth. Softstuff remained in the game—not because he was that effective but because the YJs had limited alternatives.

Leading off the sixth for the Jackets, before any chant could get going, on the first pitch, Johnny Raymond knocked a flare over the first baseman's head into short right. When the Responder right fielder failed to hustle after the ball, Raymond continued sprinting around the first-base bag and lit out for second. The right fielder's off-balance throw to second ended up down the left field line. Johnny headed for third, turned the corner, and beat the Responder short-stops' relay to home for the Yellow Jacket's first run of the season.

Calls of "Way to go, Johnny," "That's the way to get us started, John," and "Go, Johnny. Go, Johnny. Go, Johnny B. Goode," echoed down the YJ bench. Johnny attempted to deflect further praise by turning toward the plate and yelling, "Keep it goin', Larry."

Larry Chen took a more than hefty swing at the first pitch, then when the third baseman dropped back at the edge of the infield grass, he laid down an almost-perfect bunt for another base hit. On the first pitch to Stan Borison, Larry took a walking lead and easily stole second. With the count at 2–2, Stan drilled a single into left center. Chen scored and Stan took second on the throw to the plate. Sam Jackson walked on four pitches. Probably trying too hard, Alan Alford popped up to short left for the first out of the inning. With runners still on first and second, Karl McKyer (Coach/Dad) pinch hit for Randal James. His towering fly to deep center allowed both runners to advance, but it was the second out. That brought up Georgeena, who was already two for two. The Responders chose to walk her intentionally.

Well, that's a first, Mack thought as he grabbed a bat and strode to the plate. *The opponent walks a girl in order to get to me. I guess I've given 'em no reason to decide differently. We'll see. I know I can hit this guy.* Thus far, Mack had grounded out weakly to short in the third and struck out swinging at a down and away slider in the fifth. Now the bases were full of YJs, and Mack had his first clutch opportunity of the season. The Responder pitcher had basically shown him two pitches, a reasonably good but not dominating fastball and a breaking ball that he usually threw sidearm.

The first pitch to Mack was the fastball, which missed inside for ball one. The second was a breaking pitch, which broke just outside for another ball—2–0, a hitter's pitch. The fastball came in somewhere near the middle of the plate, and Mack swung with as much strength as he had. He hit the ball hard enough, but he was way in front of the pitch and drove it down the left field line about twenty feet foul. Mack stepped out of the box for a moment, oblivious to the encouragement of his teammates or the sounds from the crowd. *Well, that was stupid. All you had to do was meet that pitch square—not try and knock it to kingdom come,* he thought.

He adjusted his batting gloves and stepped back in. *I think they think I have the fastball timed pretty well now. But I don't think they think I can hit the curve, so I'm betting I'll get another one. I'm thinking there's too much thinking going on here. I just need to <u>do</u>.*

Sure enough, the pitcher stepped a bit toward third, dropped his arm angle, and sent the next pitch inside again, but Mack held back his swing and was ready when the ball spun toward the outside half of the plate. He went with the pitch, connected solidly, and drove the ball toward right center. With two out, everyone was on the move. As Mack rounded the first-base bag, he saw the center fielder holding his glove outstretched, but it got by him and caromed off the wall back toward deep center. Rounding second and out of the corner of his eye, he saw Sam Jackson scoring. Ahead of him,

Mack saw Georgeena touch third and not stop. He was about to pull up at the third base bag and was surprised to see the third base coach, Andy Wexler, making the pinwheeling motion that sent him toward home. Georgeena had her hands spread and to the left of the plate, encouraging him to slide. The ball hit the catcher's glove as his own right hand slapped the plate. The umpire's hands were also stretched flat and parallel to the ground.

Safe! A grand slam? Well, not exactly. As Mack found out later, the right fielder backing up the play had juggled the ball—giving him a couple of extra precious seconds—and then thrown wildly and missed the cutoff man. A double or a triple and an error. Still, the score was now 7–6 and just maybe they weren't done yet. Jason Denard was sent in to pinch hit for Morgan. Jason struck out on four pitches. *Well, they were done for the sixth.*

Pitching for the first time in the seventh, Denard walked the first batter he faced, but a hard-hit grounder to Chen at second resulted in a quick flip to Mack, covering second and a 4-6-3 double play. *No one in the high school league could have turned that any better!* Mack thought. Jason got the third hitter of the inning to fly out to straightaway center. In the YJ's turn at the plate, Johnny, perhaps trying to duplicate his previous race around the bases, singled again toward right center but was thrown out trying to stretch the hit into a double. Larry Chen grounded out routinely to short, and Stan Borison flew out to deep left field.

The eighth inning was a different story entirely. Jason again struggled to find the strike zone, walking the first two batters this time. The Responder cleanup hitter proceeded to double off the wall in deep left center, scoring both runners. The next batter singled to right, and the Responders had their third run of the inning. They now led 10–6. Jason pulled himself together, getting an infield pop-up followed by a strikeout and an easy grounder to Mack at short.

The bottom of the eighth started out with a bang for the Yellow Jackets when Sam Jackson sent the first pitch he saw well over the fence in straightaway left field. Josh Kelsey, batting for Alford, doubled down the right field line. Manager Karl (Coach/Dad) singled and Josh scored. The Responder relief pitcher was anything but. Georgeena drove another single through the third-short hole, and Mack walked to load the bases. Jason Denard struck out, but Johnny Raymond, swinging at the first pitch again, banged another single straight up the middle. Karl McKyer and Georgeena scored to put the Yellow Jackets ahead for the first time, 11–10. Mack slid into scoring position at third. Chen's sac fly to center gave the YJs a two-run lead. And still, they weren't done. With two out, Borison doubled to right center and Sam Jackson hit his second home run in the inning. Kelsey fouled out to the first baseman for the third out. The YJs led 14–10. The only YJ struggling that inning was Andy Wexler, who was trying to keep the score book accurately.

The rest of the game was almost anticlimactic. The Responders made some noise with three straight singles in the top of the ninth. They scored one but that was it—an infield fly, a grounder gloved by Josh at third, and a final well-hit drive run down by Johnny Raymond in deep left center. Final score: Yellow Jackets 14, First Responders 11.

The pitching had been relatively disastrous, but the offense had come through when it had to and they had won their first game. Mack walked off the field with mixed emotions. He felt good about his one really clutch hit in the sixth, but he had only gone one for five and a walk. His defense had been solid (except for the first inning), but he hadn't had any tough chances. As for his assessment about the commercial league competition, he decided to withhold judgment. He had now only seen one team besides his own. He told himself he was trying to be objective, but even to himself, he admitted his thoughts were pretty arrogant for someone who had only gone 1–5 (and a walk).

CHAPTER 12

All Kinds of Prejudice

Mack was helping his dad collect and bag up the bats, balls, helmets, and extra catcher's gear and not paying much attention to anything other than his internal world, when he swung the canvas bat bag over his shoulder and nearly knocked John Raymond on to his backside.

"Oops, sorry. Didn't see ya for a second." There was a pause—awkward city—then he said, "Oh yeah, we were going to get together. I wasn't thinking today."

"Okay then. Let's make it another time," Johnny said as he started to walk away.

Mack took a deep breath. He was of two minds—part of him wanting to go home but the other part seeing how disappointed John was. *Damn it. Why can't I just say no sometimes? I am not responsible for how he feels. I can do whatever I really want to, can't I? He probably doesn't care anyway. It's just that—*

"John, wait up." A brief check-in with coach/Dad and he said, "You got wheels, John?"

John Raymond said he did. They walked toward the parking lot together. At one point, Mack threw an arm around John's shoulder and said, "Hey, good game. I didn't realize you were that fast."

John Raymond glanced at him with a puzzled look on his face. "Really?" he said.

"Really."

They sat in the car for a moment before Mack asked where John wanted to go and quickly regretted it.

"How about the Spoon? You work there sometimes, right?"

Now might have been the time to suggest some other place but why? Why not? he thought.

"Sure, the Spoon it is. Nothing like ice cream to go with base-ball talk."

"You're going to think I'm really weird, but I don't actually like ice cream that much."

Mack did think that was indeed weird, but it also provided a rationale for going somewhere else.

"Oh no," said John, "the Spoon is fine. Love your hot chocolate."

An awkward silence ensued as John drove the mile or so to the restaurant. When they walked in, the Spoon seemed quieter than usual to Mack. Or had it suddenly gotten quiet when they entered? *Talk about weird. Must be my imagination.* It was about the dinner hour, and there were several vacant tables. They grabbed one about halfway down the wall across the room from the coffee bar.

"All right," said a familiar voice making its way across the room. "Glad to see the Yellow Jacket postgame gathering includes the Spoon today," said Randal James as he walked quickly from the bar to their table. "Great game, you guys. What'll you have? It's on the house."

"Oh, just put it on my tab," said Mack with a grin. "I'll have a small hot fudge sundae and a large glass of water. I'm trying to watch my waistline. You wanna stick with the hot chocolate, John?"

"Sure."

Randal spoke the order to Susan who was cleaning up behind the bar. Then he glanced around the dining area. "Seems like business has slowed down for the night. Everyone in here has been served. Mind if I join you for a few minutes?"

"Well," started John.

"No problem," said Mack at the same time. John shrugged. Randal grabbed a chair.

Soon, the three of them were into a recap of the ball game. Before long, talk morphed into favorite major league teams and who was expected to have an up or down year. Almost before they knew it, Randal had taken over the conversation, dwelling on his long-term boyhood connection to the San Francisco Giants and his favorite players: catcher Buster Posey ("From the first of his career, he looked like he was barely out of middle school and probably only shaved every three days.") and Tim Lincecum, a pitcher neither Mack nor John remembered. ("Scrawny guy but man, could he really throw smoke.") As he was in the middle of his reminiscences of the Giants great teams of the nineties, Randal stopped, suddenly aware that both younger guys—while nodding like they cared—were really not paying that close attention.

"Okay," he said. "I realize I just hijacked the conversation and you guys probably have teenage stuff you want to talk about. Besides," he added as Mack started to protest, "I've got my stuff to do to get ready for the evening rush." There wasn't much to say to that.

As Randal walked back across the room, both guys took a deep breath, a pair of sighs actually—Mack because he thought maybe he was ready to head home and didn't want to assume John Raymond felt the same. *But what was John's sigh all about? Do I want to know?* he thought.

It was John who broke the silence, "So have you always been called Mack?"

"Ever since I can remember, which is a bit odd I guess since my dad could also be Mack and he's always been Karl. Then again, to be honest, I really don't like my actual given name: Francis. But there you go. Francis is a family name going back about four generations. But what about you? Do you want to be called John or Johnny or Jonathan?"

"Tell you what. I'll call you Mack if you call me Johnny. John just sounds too formal and Jonathan even worse."

"All right. Settled. It's Johnny then and Mack." There was another awkward pause.

Then with a nod across the room toward Randal, Johnny asked, "What's he like to work for?"

"Oh, great. No complaints. He's a good guy. Cares about us kids—both him and his wife, Susan. Actually, I didn't know he was so in to baseball. It was a bit of a shock when my dad told me Randal was on the team. But until the last half hour, he seemed to be good at keeping job and baseball separate. I don't know. I think it's going to work out. I wasn't very sure about the whole Yellow Jackets business, ya know, playing baseball with my dad more than Randal and not playing for the high school team. Say, how come you don't play for Lincoln? You're sure good enough. But then again, I'm not sure the Lincoln coaches are great at assessing baseball talent—"

Mack stopped there, rather thinking he had said too much or at least more than he intended. It wasn't like him to *run off at the mouth—usually only when he was feeling anxious.* Was he? Why was he feeling anxious? But John's follow-up question still caught him by surprise.

"So is your dad a pretty tolerant guy, would you say?" *Where did that come from?* Mack thought.

He reassessed. "Uh, yeah, I guess. I don't know if any kid can be very objective about their own parents. But, geez, at least I can't complain. My mom, uh, maybe a little less. She's on my case more often than my dad, but actually, I don't know why I said that. They're usually on the same page. It's only been like recently, like I think she really needs to get back to teaching. She's been looking for a job, but so far, nothing except subbing and she can't do much of that with her other part-time work. It feels a lot longer to me, but we've only been here in Columbia City for about nine months—" About then, it seemed to Mack that Johnny Raymond's eyes were about to glaze over and he stopped midsentence. "Why'd you ask about my dad?"

"Hell, I don't know. I just thought, well, I just thought I should know what I'm up against."

"What you're up against. I don't get it."

"You mean you never have to deal with prejudice, bias, hatred— that sort of thing?"

"No, not really. I suppose you could say I've been lucky that way. It's not like I'm Black or Chinese or somethin'. Actually, that sounds kind of cringy. I can't believe I said that. I just mean—well, like you and me both—it's nothin' to be proud of, White privilege and all that." *What is this about? I'm sounding like a lame doofus or something*, he thought.

"There are all kinds of prejudice."

"Well, yeah, so?" Johnny said nothing in response. To Mack, it seemed like something in Johnny Raymond had shut down and he couldn't imagine what he had said to make that happen.

"Um, I don't know as this has anything to do with what we've been talking about, but I haven't asked you about that ballpark chant that seemed to upset you. What was that about—if you don't mind my asking?"

"You really don't know?" Mack shook his head.

"Well, I'll be damned. This is certainly not turning out how I thought it might." He paused and added, "You don't know that I'm gay?"

"You're what? You're g———"

"I'm gay, but you don't have to announce it to the world. Although most of my world knows. Randal certainly knows. And since he's the only other person here, I guess maybe you are free to shout it out as loudly as you want." And he mimicked, "Johnny Rainbow. Johnny Rainbow."

"Well now, don't I feel stupid. I'm sorry. And no, I didn't know. Oh, I suppose part of me wondered a little. But I guess I figured that wasn't any of my business."

"It's all right. No need to worry. I won't embarrass you by trying to hang out or buddy up. Fact is as far as I'm concerned, this date never happened."

"So you thought of this as a date. And that's why you were asking about my dad's tolerance, etc. I get it. I really do."

But did he? On the outside, Mack knew he appeared much calmer than he felt on the inside where he was suddenly wondering, *How can I get out of this without hurting Johnny's feelings? What if someone sees us driving together? Should I call my dad and ask him to pick me up? Oh crap, what if one of the kids that was in here earlier decides to tell the world, "I saw Mack McKyer and Johnny Raymond on a date together."*

"Johnny," he said, "you're going to think this is dumb, but I've never really known someone who is gay before."

"Someone you knew was gay you mean. It's not like all of us go through life announcing our sexual orientation to the world. Come on. Let's get out of here. I'll take you home and hopefully no one else will see us." *Guess he kind of saw right through me with that one*, Mack thought. Johnny got up, grabbed his sweatshirt, and headed for the door.

There was a brief moment of further hesitation. *I could always walk home. It's only about three miles*, he thought. He felt, well, furtive would be a word as they waved goodbye to Randal and made their way across the street where John had parked. When two other cars passed going opposite directions in *broad daylight*, Mack felt exposed. How would he explain himself if indeed someone he knew saw him and Johnny together?

Mack settled into the front passenger side of Johnny's car. He was tempted to scrunch down below the level of the door window but better form prevailed. As Johnny pulled away into traffic, he put both hands to the sides of his head and stared at the dashboard. He found no further words for the moment. Johnny, however, was not through.

He said, "Do you remember that day—that school day—when we saw each other across the street there?" He pointed. "I was underneath the theater marquee, and you were by that corner lamppost. But I had seen you at the movie. I knew who you were, even if you didn't know me. Who at Lincoln doesn't know Mack McKyer—star athlete? I don't know—stupid of me, I guess—but I thought you must be gay too. Who else, I reasoned, would want to see that movie—especially on a school day when no one else was around?" Mack scrunched a little lower in the seat but felt like he had to say something.

"What do you want me to say? I can't. There's a whole long story about how I ended up at that movie that day, but I'm not gay—if you need me to say so out loud or something. And I'll say one other thing: I'm kind of blown away here. I don't know what I need to do or even what I want to do. I think I'd still like to be your friend, but I don't know what that would look like."

"You mean you want to be my friend but you don't want anyone else to know, right?"

"No, I mean literally I don't know."

"That's an asshole response, if you don't mind my use of the language."

The rest of the drive was in silence. As Mack got out of the car, he started to say some kind of—he wasn't sure what—*maybe thankyou for the ride or something equally inane. But* Johnny floored the gas pedal and screeched around the corner with the door still hanging open.

CHAPTER 13

Avoidance

Mack still had a lot of thinking-reflecting time left of the weekend after Saturday night's debacle, but the truth of the matter was he didn't want to think about it—whatever it was. So he didn't. There were, after all, a lot of things he had to think and/or do something about—like schoolwork or his part-time job or keeping up with his friends, how the baseball season was going, and his dating life. Actually, the last two were a little too close to what he didn't want to think about. So he didn't—much.

On Sunday afternoon, he did spend a couple of hours at the central area community center where he knew he could always find a pickup b-ball, as in basketball, game. Sure enough, it was good to connect with Nate, Skye, and the guys and play the macho style of ball that was the central city tradition. No, he didn't need to prove his manhood to anyone. That wasn't why he was there, was it?

And that night, he finally got around to texting, then calling Elana.

"Hey, how ya doin'?"

"Hey yourself. It's been a while."

"Not that long."

"Two weeks unless you count the waves across the classroom."

"And the staying-in-touch texts."

"Oh yes, the staying-in-touch texts."

"Yeah, you're right. I'm sorry. My bad. I've been thinkin' about you a lot, though. Does that count?"

"Depends what you've been thinkin'."

"You must have some idea." *Sheesh, I am bad at this flirting stuff,* he thought.

"You <u>are</u> bad." *And now she is reading my mind.*

"Probably. Hey, how about we hang out for a few hours this week?" *That's leaving it wide open.*

And so it went. For better or worse, he now had a date Friday. *Got to figure out something romantic. Can't just go straight to some parking spot. If the weather's okay, maybe we could go for a hike somewhere and get lost for a couple of hours. See, everybody, I'm a man. Attractive girls want to go out with me—at least one. This is really stupid, ya know.*

*****

School that week was interesting. Mack saw Johnny a couple of times every day—from a distance. He tried direct eye contact, looking for at least an acknowledging nod or wave, but Johnny either didn't or pretended not to see him. In the back of his mind, the questions that kept occurring were the following: *Why am I concerned here?* and *Why am I making Johnny's thing my problem? So the guy doesn't want to be friends. Everyone doesn't have to be your friend, Mack. So he's gay and I'M NOT. Right? Of course, I'm not. I like girls. I've always liked girls, even though I sure as hell don't understand them at all. What's the big deal about sex anyway? I mean there's a lot more to life than sexuality, isn't there?*

Of course, the back-of-his-mind remained hidden from everyone else and—even, at times, he had to admit—*from himself.* How could you talk about this stuff to anyone? People would think you were gay—even when you weren't at all gay. Couldn't you just like someone and not be in love or lust? Did he like Johnny? Well, yeah. Before things turned out as they had on Saturday, he had thought John Raymond was a nice guy who he would probably like to get to know better. So what had changed really?

What Mack actually wanted to do was talk to his *friend* Katy. That seemed more difficult these days now that she was dating his *friend* Tad. Quite suddenly, he felt cautious using the word he had always used with no real thought in the matter. Anyway, the few moments sitting behind Katy in homeroom weren't long enough or private enough for the kind of conversation he needed to have with someone. And they couldn't go on another one of those semi-date dates they had managed in the past, could they?

Katy had seemed okay with it the last time, but, *I mean I don't need a jealous Tad wanting a piece of me—to say nothing of a jealous Elana.* Maybe between his job and baseball and their social commitments, they'd be able to find time for a walk and a talk in one of Columbia City's fine parks. *Sheesh. What's this about wandering about in the great outdoors? Hikes with Elana. Strolls in the park with Katy, heck. Who knows? Maybe even a down-the-road beach romp with Lisa someday.* Must be the weather. Like Kerry is always saying, "So many women, so little time." *Ha! Ha! I can't believe how crazy making this all is.*

Then there was school itself, of course. More to the point— school in May. *Did anyone ever actually learn anything in May?* Closing in on a year—a whole school year with all these people. *I know a lot of them now, but there are a whole lot more I don't know. And how many are actually my friends? Sometimes it seemed like fifty, maybe seventy-five. But who's counting? Other times one or two seems a stretch. Two thousand kids—young people, teenagers, probably one hundred staff. And everyone—EVERYONE—trying to figure out his or her or their place in the universe. Math, history, science, English, etc. and none of them teaching me how to be a friend*, he thought. That, he concluded not for the first time, was totally up to him.

Monday drifted by with no new insight or resolution. Mack went through the motions, doing what he had to do or most of it anyway. That night, he woke up two or three times with disturbing dreams. On Tuesday morning, he didn't remember the explicit content but knew at some level that they were related to his sexual identity. He chose the easier path this time. He simply refused to think about any of it *for the time being.* It was Tuesday and a baseball game day. *Focus, Mack, focus. The Civil War Recovery Period, Shakespeare, chemistry, trig—that's enough*, he thought.

But now, on his way to the ball field, he had to work to control his scattered thoughts. *Eye on the ball, watching it into the glove and off the bat. Focus.*

For that one Tuesday in early May, things on the field seemed to work—at least for Mack and the YJs. He went three for four, two singles and a double into the left center field gap. He cleanly handled three routine chances at short, including the start of a second double play, McKyer to Chen to James. And the team as a whole played well enough to win their second game in a row. The hitting star of the day was Alan Alford who was also three for four, but his came with runners on base in the second and fifth innings. One of Alford's hits was a double and one a home run for a total of five RBI. Mack was also impressed when Softstuff Morgan, pitching on three days' rest, managed to last into the eighth inning, serving up a steady diet of well-placed slow curves and changeups. Mack continued to wonder why the opposing hitters were fooled so badly by the off-speed pitches when Morgan's fastball was not a lot faster than his changeup but so it seemed. The Swedish Meatballs managed a five-run rally in the eighth off Denard. Nevertheless, the YJs had picked up enough early runs to hold the other team off, finishing at 11–7.

Mack occasionally glanced in Johnny Raymond's direction, either down the bench when the team was on offence or out toward center field. He thought he caught Johnny looking his way a couple of times, too, but perhaps it was his imagination. Neither of them went out of their way to say even a word or two. *Perhaps that's just the way it's going to be. Could be not a little awkward if it goes on all season?*

Still, Mack's thoughts went, *maybe it's all for the best. Can a straight person actually be friends with a gay guy? Better said or thought, can a guy like me be friends with a guy like Johnny?*

By the time the next day—Wednesday—rolled around, Mack decided he would go to his it-just-doesn't-matter space. That was a place in his head that he liked to wander in when he figured either no one could possibly understand him (including himself) so he could pretend he didn't care what anyone (including himself) thought or said. "It just doesn't matter. It just doesn't matter." *Maybe I heard that phrase in an old movie sometime* (see *Meatballs* with Bill Murray). *Ah, well,* he thought.

Unfortunately, his wandering attitude did not serve him well when schoolwork—actually, any kind of work—was involved. At least twice—once in history and once in trig—the teacher had to say his name three times before getting his attention and of course, he had no idea what he had been asked. Mack did not think voicing his meme would work well with either teacher. So he wisely said nothing and resigned himself to a low class-participation mark. Then there was his unfortunate afternoon shift at the Spoon when he couldn't seem to get anyone's order right, spilled a diet Coke all over a customer's dress—fortunately, he didn't know her—and twice gave away his tip money in extra change. *But hey, it just doesn't matter.*

Thursday was better. Perhaps it was the fuller previous nights' sleep sans disturbing dreams—at least any he remembered. He also finally had a homeroom opportunity to check in with Katy. It started profoundly enough. *Yeah, right.*

Mack (tapping K's shoulder) said, "Hey." He tried to smile. At least it was more than a grimace.

Katy (turning halfway around in her seat) said, "Hey." Blink, blink, blink. "What's up?"

"Looks like Fletcher's running a little late again today."

"Teachers' conference still going, I heard. Something about some kids being bullied after school."

"I hadn't heard about it, but hey," he said again.

"Hey back, you anxious about somethin'?"

"Reading my mind again?"

"What mind?"

"Well, there's that I suppose. Good point."

"Right. Now you're gonna play the humble card."

"What can I say? That's me. But just makes it harder askin——"

"Okay, now you got me."

"That easy, huh? Look, I need to bend your ear again. Sometime soon?"

"Anytime. My ears to your words. Go ahead."

"Not now." And his voice dropped to a whisper. "I need to be private with this."

"Uh, okay. What didya have in that humble mind?"

Mack sighed. "Maybe this wasn't such a good idea." Katy then made her own quite-exaggerated sigh and rolled her eyes—twice in case he didn't see it the first time. She didn't have to say anything further.

"I was thinking maybe we could"—pause for idea to surface in mind—"go for walk in Woodland Park Sunday?"

"Mack, is this a date?"

Before he recognized that those were familiar words from their history and that she was definitely teasing him, he blurted out, "No, no, of course not. I mean you've got Tad now and I. Sheesh, Katy."

Her broad smile brought him back to the real world. "Just kidding. And you've got Elana still—this week." *Was that a subtle slam on Elana or me or both of us or?*

They agreed to meet at the Main Washington Avenue entrance of the park at two. She told him she would let Tad know. He said he didn't think that was a great idea. He did not think he would say anything to Elana or anyone else for that matter.

But there it was—date or not, no, not, definitely not. *Tad, you hear me, right?* Regardless, Katy had a way about her. Knowing they would have that time together ahead of him, there was more of a spring in his step the rest of the day. He had something to look forward to in a weird way—something besides baseball or he had nearly forgotten, his date with Elana on Friday. *Thanks, Katy. Stuff matters again. I wonder what I would be feeling like if things were reversed and I was going on a real date with Katy on Friday and going on a walk and talk with Elana on Sunday. Better not go down that road right now. Probably never*, he thought.

CHAPTER 14

Two Dates

Friday was a teacher continuing education day, so no classes and a free day for students. It had seemed like such a good idea when he first thought of it a couple of weeks earlier. However, for reasons he was not yet ready to name, Mack was not looking forward to his basically all-day date with Elana. He almost hoped the weather would deteriorate into something cold, windy, and wet, giving him an excuse to call things off. Then again, she would likely expect him to come up with a bad weather option. At least with the hike, he had a plan, such as it was. There was a trail Elana said she had taken in the past. They would need to drive outside the city about twenty-five miles to the trailhead, then walk about three miles through some old growth forest to an alpine lake where they could picnic and maybe take a swim if the weather stayed warm.

What could possibly go wrong? It sounded like an ideal thing to do with someone you loved. *Okay, maybe that's it. Maybe? Could be? Do I love Elana? Now there's a ridiculous question. And did that really have to be the point? Why not just see some beautiful scenery and enjoy nature? And make out a bit? Uh, yeah? Am I trying to talk myself into something here? What is the matter with you, McKyer? Lighten up for god's sakes!*

The day had not cooperated with Mack's ambivalence—bright sun, hardly a cloud in the sky all day long. No excuses. Though briefly, he did think that it was also a great day for baseball. Nonetheless, when he knocked on Elana's door, he had to pretend to an excitement he did not feel. Well, yes, it *was* a great day for baseball, but he was about to embark on a very private several hours with a really attractive girl who he knew liked him a lot. And he liked her. So what is the problem?

When she came to the door, Elana was obviously ready to go—even a bit anxious it seemed. She yelled a goodbye to her mom, and almost exactly like the other couple of times he had picked her up, she raced to the car and jumped in. When Mack followed more slowly and sat behind the wheel, Elana leaned over, kissed him on the cheek, and said immediately, "Let's get this show on the road."

The first two thirds of the car trip to the trailhead were pleasant enough. Elana certainly kept up her end of things. As long as they stayed with the topics of school, difficult teachers, other kids they liked (or didn't), and choir, school play (Elana), or baseball (Mack), there was generally enough material. There were only a couple of awkward silences. And those were mostly in Mack's court. The pleasantness ended with what Mack thought was a rather innocent question—questions actually.

He began with "You know I don't know anything about your family." There was a pause, no verbal response. "So what about them? Brothers? Sisters? Do both your mom and dad work? What do they do?"

"I don't really want to talk about them." There was another major pause.

"Hey, I only asked 'cause you never talk about them—at least with me."

"Sure, I do."

"Uh, no, you don't. All I know is you've got an older sister. You mentioned her once. She lives in California I think you said."

"So you see. I do talk about them. And actually, I have two older sisters."

"All right, already. You don't wanna go there. I get it. I'm not gonna force you or something. It's kinda like one of those things everybody talks about."

"Well, I'm not everybody I guess." Again, there was an awkward pause. "But if we're going to talk about families, you go ahead. I don't know much about yours either."

"That's not true and you know it. You know my dad manages the Sporting Goods store and my mom's looking for an elementary school teaching job. And you know my sister Jana is in her last year of middle school and will be at Lincoln next year. I may not have said the actual words, but most of the time, we all get along pretty good. Jana and I didn't used to, but it's been better the last couple of years—when she minds her own business anyway. When we were younger, we all used to do lots of stuff together (not so much any-more but sometimes), and they still almost always come to my games (at least my dad but also the girls) most of the time."

"Maybe you'll think this is strange then, but it almost sounds like you all love each other."

"Uh, yeah, sorta. Yeah, I guess we do."

Then after yet another pause and in a quiet monotone, Elana said, "My parents don't give a shit about me. And I don't give a shit about them."

"Oh."

The last ten minutes of the car trip seemed to take another thirty. When Elana spoke again, it was to say, "Slow down. There's the sign on the left: Parking lot's a short drive through the trees."

It wasn't a really easy hike—on the way, lots of ups and downs with the ups lasting longer. The trail itself was a mix of smooth dirt and pine needles with only occasional roots, rocks, and fallen trees. Walking behind her most of the way, Mack enjoyed the views of mountains, trees, valleys, and Elana's backside. About two and a half hours from the start, they emerged from a last forested slope and stood on a barren hill-shaped rock formation, looking down on the reflective waters of a mountain lake. They had passed a few fellow hikers on their way up. But for the moment, there was not another soul in sight.

Mack wasn't sure what he was looking for but decided it was definitely going to be away from the main trail, so taking Elana's hand, they walked beside the lake for about a quarter of a mile. They stopped near a small stream merging into the lake. There was a grassy area about twenty feet wide between the lake and the narrow path around the lake surrounded by large evergreen trees, which gave at least an illusion of privacy. There was a small firepit close to the lakeshore. The air was a bit chilly—perhaps a combination of the higher elevation and the mountain born breeze off the water. The thought of a swim was definitely out, but building a fire appealed to both of them—for some warmth and to roast the marshmallows Elana had brought for s'mores.

Mack went in search of some firewood, while Elana spread a blanket and a picnic lunch of sandwiches, cut veggies, sodas, and a box of cookies. About five minutes later, Mack returned with an armful of wood and built a small fire. They finished eating, except for s'more munching and sipping the last of the sodas.

"It's so beautiful. Thanks for being willing to spend all this time getting here. I'm glad you thought of that," Elana said, pointing to the fire. "I didn't think we'd need it, but I am kind of cold."

"Yeah. This high in the mountains this time of year you never know."

"Okay, and how would you know, Mr. Midwest who's never been to the mountains at all?"

"Hey, I only said I haven't been to these mountains. My family traveled around at bit, even when we lived in Iowa. I've been to Colorado and even up into the Canadian Rockies a couple of times. Oops. Sorry. I mentioned family again."

"Yes, you did. And I'll forgive you if you'll slide over closer here and help me get warm."

Mack heard that as the invitation it was and before long getting warm became something more. He discovered several things he had not known for sure until that afternoon. *Yeah, someday I'll think this was pretty dumb but so be it.*

As he felt the length of Elana's body on his own, the first thought he had—though thought was not quite the right word, more like a counterintuitive feeling—was this: *I don't love this girl. I like her but.* And his second thought/feeling was this: *I don't care. This feels really good and I don't want to stop.* And when he was able to think again, it was with a rather unexpected anger at his parents coupled with this: *It is quite possible, even likely, that guys could want to make love to a person even when they did not love that person.* He wasn't near as sure about girls.

That's the thing with his parents. In their well-intended—he reminded himself—advice regarding sex, they always seem to end up saying that love and sex go together. He hadn't really questioned that until this moment. And it threw him enough to put the emotional brakes on when a strong part of him did not want to do that at all.

He physically rolled Elana over, held her face, looked into her eyes—she did have beautiful eyes—kissed her softly, and managed to stand up without embarrassing himself too much, mumbling, like some B-movie guy, "I need a drink."

"What?"

"I need a drink. We're out of soda, but I can use a pop can." He picked that up and without further thought, walked over to the stream and dipped the can in until it was nearly full.

He drank a large swallow just as Elana called out, "What about Guardia? Do you want to get sick?"

Mack shrugged and reloaded his soda can, but as he was pulling away from the stream, the hand he was leaning on to keep from getting wet slipped on the side of the stream bank. He dropped the can and at the same time, thrust his other hand into the water to keep from falling. He didn't feel much at first, but when he brought that second hand out of the water, his palm was slit wide open and bleeding profusely. Then he felt the pain. For a moment, looking at his hand, he also felt like vomiting. But yelling, "Ow," and an expletive, he ripped off a corner of his shirt and pressed it into the wound. When the makeshift bandage turned a solid red, he finally asked Elana if she had brought a first-aid kit. He sure hadn't. She began to rummage around in her backpack and eventually came up with a couple of paper towels and some twine.

"Will this help?"

"Better than nothing I guess." With her assistance, Mack doubled over both paper towels and they tied a couple of pieces of twine around his hand. "Now where were we?" he offered.

"Oh no, you don't. We are going to get out of here as soon as possible and get you to an ER before you bleed to death. And I don't want to be the one to call your parents if we don't make it."

Later, Mack would wonder if he had managed to unconsciously sabotage what for a moment had seemed the inevitable deepening of their relationship. In the moments he provided limited one-hand assistance to packing up their stuff, all he was aware of thinking sarcastically was *What a lovely way to end the day. I cannot believe what I just did.*

The hike back down to the trailhead was anticlimactic, except it seemed to take forever, his hand was hurting like blazes, and the paper towels were nearly soaked clear through by the time they arrived at the car. Fortunately, Elana was okay driving. For his part, Mack was feeling guilty on so many different levels that he wanted to hide under the picnic blanket and block out the world. The hand pain wouldn't quite let him do that, but neither was Elana willing to listen to "such garbage. This is not your fault, Francis Allen McKyer. You slipped on a rock. We didn't get to stay as long as we wanted to, but there will be other times. Meanwhile, just go to sleep and pretend I'm not going twenty miles per hour over the limit."

All he had to say was "Cool it. I haven't lost that much blood. And I'd prefer not to lose any more if you take one of these curves too fast."

"Ha. Ha."

Using his good hand, Mack called his parents on their way back to the city. Unfortunately, the first words out of his mouth were "There's been an accident." Of course, that was enough for his mom. "Among the worst words a parent can hear" was her later explanation. He was afraid she had fainted and didn't hear his "I'm sorry, Mom. It's no big deal." In a panic, she had given the phone to his dad to whom he said what had actually happened and that they would be going to the hospital ER to see if he needed stitches in his hand.

They arrived at the hospital. Mack's parents were already there looking for them. His dad was his usual quiet, controlled self. His mom, acting as though she expected Mack to keel over at any moment, ordered him to sit down. He hoped to introduce them to

Elana and perhaps have a nice get-acquainted conversation, but a nurse interrupted and asked him to follow her into one of the treatment rooms. His over-the-shoulder suggestion that maybe his dad could drive Elana home met with a stony stare from Elana who said rather forcefully, "I'll hang out here in case you do something else stupid. I wouldn't want to miss it. Besides, your parents are nice people. Remember."

When Mack did return to the waiting area with seven stitches in his palm and a very large bandage that made him look, he felt, like he might have managed to have amputated half of his hand, the three of them appeared to have forgotten all about him. They were leaning in toward one another, intent on what the others were saying. He stood there for a minute or two before they saw him. Though they all seemed to be feeling quite natural about things, it was a strange moment for him. Briefly, he imagined a future in which they were all family. What a very weird day it had been in so many ways. He really didn't want to think about it. All he wanted to do was go home, take a pain pill, and go to bed.

*****

Mack spent most of Saturday feeling sorry for himself. His hand still hurt and he didn't feel like using only one hand on his computer. The meds helped but made him feel drowsy. He didn't even feel up to going to the Yellow Jacket game. So it was a TV-and-sleep day. When the rest of the family returned from the game, he made himself listen to his dad's recount of their 10–8 win over the Swedish Meatballs. He couldn't even work up a humorous quip like "So much for a good pasta" or "I guess the meatballs didn't meet enough balls" or some such. What a nothing day. He even thought about calling Katy and canceling their Sunday afternoon date. But he didn't.

With the exception of a botched shaving job while using his left hand, Sunday started out on a better note. After his—*slightly* overdone—complaints about his hand pain and not being able to get a good night sleep, the rest of the family let him alone while they traipsed off to church. With everyone else gone for the morning, the house was mercifully quiet. Somebody had left him some eggs to warm up in the microwave and a whole homemade cinnamon roll. Even with one hand, he was able to manage a pleasant breakfast on the backyard deck. While sipping a cup of hot chocolate (reheated twice), he was even able to catch up on the Major League Baseball standings and his reading-related homework (in that order). He intentionally tried not to think about where he wanted the walk-and-talk session with Katy to go. And he also carefully avoided too much thinking about the post-picnic, pre-accident part of his date with Elana.

The park where he and Katy had decided to meet was an easy twenty-minute walk from Mack's place. He left in plenty of time to arrive early enough that she wouldn't have to wait. He found an empty park bench near the rose garden entrance, sat, and fiddled with his phone, checking social media posts. He was rereading a personal message from Elana and trying to decide how to respond when he felt the feathery touch of a hand on the back of his neck. He barely checked himself from jumping several feet straight up, then quickly went into of-course-it's-you mode before Katy could say, "Gotcha."

For a moment, Mack felt anxious—more so than he expected. Hadn't they already clarified that this was not a date? Hadn't they said they would mention this outing to their respective boyfriend, girlfriend? Well, Katy had, anyway. Somehow, it hadn't come up between him and Elana. And this was hardly a private, hidden, clandestine meeting. It was the clear light of day in a public place where they might in fact see any number of people they knew. *Oh right, that was the point.*

So they walked and talked. (And of course, he explained why the large bandage on the hand.) And eventually, Mack got tired of looking for school newspaper reporters or any other embarrassing people. Well, maybe it was Katy's bemused question.

"Seen anybody you know yet?"

"Uh, no. Why? Don't you ever worry about what other people think?"

"Then maybe you should have worn a disguise: dark glasses, a hat pulled down over the top half of your face."

"Now why would I do that?"

"Come on, Mack. You're acting like you don't want to be seen with me. That's not very flattering to a girl, you know—even if it's not a date."

"No, of course not. Is it that obvious?" She then did quite an accurate mimic of his turning this way and that, eyes darting in all directions.

"Oh, okay, yes. I'm being stupid. But it is about me—not about you. Any guy would feel good walkin' around with you I mean, oh, you know what I mean."

"Maybe, so then look me in the eyes for once if you can without tripping over your own two feet and tell me what the heck is going on—same rules as in times past—just between you and me."

They stopped about halfway across a footbridge over one of the many ponds in the park and leaned—not touching—on a railing, glancing toward the water and a momma duck leading her newborn ducklings for a swim. Mack took a deep breath.

He muttered quietly, "Sometimes I think I'd rather be a duck."
"A what?"

"A duck, you know, like those. Yellow, white, and purply with optional stripe, floating through life. Nothin' to worry about, just stay in line. Follow Mom. Eat a bug or two if she says it's okay. No worries. All of life is a bug banquet. Grow up. Become a big duck. Have little ducks who follow you in line. Repeat."

"Well, there are hawks and dogs and winter in the great out of doors and sometimes hunters with shotguns."

"Yeah, yeah, yeah, but at least there aren't any gay ducks."

"Uh, you know this for sure?" He looked at her. "Okay, I'm guessing this conversation is going to take a human turn in a moment."

"Right. So there's this guy."

"Johnny Raymond." Mack stared at her for a moment.

"You know him."

"I do. He's a senior. Sings in the choir. Been in a couple of school drama productions. Likes baseball. In fact, doesn't he play on your team?"

"Sometimes you know too much for your own good."

"Probably. But Johnny Raymond. What's he got to do with you—besides being baseball teammates?"

"Geezes, Katy. Johnny's gay."

"Yeah. I know that too. So what?"

"So I like him."

"I like him too. He's always seemed like a nice guy. Even when some of the more macho guys tease him, he doesn't let it bother him."

"I don't know about that. Some 'fans' at our last games are yelling 'Johnny Rainbow, Johnny Rainbow,'" said Mack, mimicking the high-voiced cry from the crowd. That bothers him, I'm sure, though I didn't understand why the first time I heard them.

"This still doesn't sound like anything having to do with you."

"I'll spell it out. Johnny and I went out to the Spoon after one of last weeks' games. He actually thought we were out on a date—or at least wondered."

"Were you?"

"No. No. Are you serious? I'm not gay!"

"Then—"

"Katy, I want to be his friend—not his lover."

"And that's a rough go—especially in the crowds you travel in."

"What d' ya mean by that?"

"You know what I mean. Jocks must be among the most homophobic people that walk the face of the earth."

"Well, that's a prejudicial statement if I ever heard one. Repeat. I want to be his friend—not his lover. And apparently, he is not interested."

"So your native charm doesn't work with guys, huh?"

"You are so helpful today."

"Sorry. Let me try again. Here, you and I are. We like each other. We're both reasonably attractive people. But we have chosen to be friends, not lovers. And—believe me in this, Mack—not everyone can manage to pull that off. Maybe Johnny can't pull that off. At least in some—maybe most—respects, gay people aren't any different from straight. If they can't be but want to be lovers with a particular person, some—probably most—can't handle being friends."

"Hmm. Not bad. How much do I owe you?" She punched him in the arm. "One more thing—in the area of friends being honest with friends. And you have to promise you won't laugh."

"Cross my heart and hope to die. Now that's stupid. Where did I learn that?"

"Likewise. The remaining thought was—now no big thing, just a small part of me, but here it is—the encounter with Johnny. For a moment, I had to ask myself. And you're going to laugh inside. I know it. I had to ask, 'What if I am gay and just never realized it?' See, you're going to think this is stupid. But how does anyone know for sure, huh?"

"You're doing it again."

"Doing what?"

"Not looking me in the eyes. I'm not sure, but it seems like you don't really care what I think. Or maybe that you don't want to know or you want to know but only so you can discount what I have to say."

"Gees. That's convoluted—even for you." Mack smiled to take any sting out of his words.

"I didn't even know you knew that big of a word."

Mack took another deep breath and with both hands, turned Katy's head so he could look deeply into her eyes.

"Do you think I'm gay?"

"Well, the Q in LGTBQ usually means queer, but I guess it could mean questioning."

"I've heard both."

"But damn it, Mack. If you are gay, you are the most closeted, least obvious gay person in the world. And let me go out on another real limb here. What I think is not very important."

"Yeah, I know." And he laughed. "I do know something sometimes. And in this, it is about me and what I think."

"Duh."

"But as usual, you're not telling me what to do."

"Ding, ding. You win the prize."

"Not even a hint?"

"One more try. Mack, you are a good guy. You just need to do what <u>you</u> believe is right."

"Okay then. Thanks. <u>You</u>'ve been a lot of help."

Katy shook her head slowly. "McKyer, you are one strange dude sometimes. So you ready to get out of here? I <u>do</u> need to get back to my real life fairly soon—one that sometimes makes sense to me."

Katy started to move down the path away from the bridge but stopped and looked Mack full in the face. "Friends?" she said, reaching out her hand.

Mack took her hand with his unbandaged one, holding on for a couple of seconds longer than Elana would have appreciated.

"Friends," he said.

As they walked together toward the park entrance, Mack's left hand was inconveniently in his pockets. Katy took his arm and for a moment. It felt—to Mack anyway—that they were walking down an aisle from one life to the next. *Strange for sure. Remember these moments. This moment. Somehow that felt important.*

"You sure you don't want a lift home?" Katy asked.

"No, I need some alone time to think about what you said and what you didn't say."

She smiled. Mack kept walking.

CHAPTER 15

An Opportunity Surfaces

Mack, you fool! What in the heck did you expect? He knocked the dirt out of his cleats and stepped back into the batter's box. *Maybe it will be different this time.* His first bat-on-ball contact since practice the previous Thursday had been off the end of the bat—a slow roller back to the mound. And, *my oh my*, his hand hurt. With determination—and hoping the first had been a fluke—he met the ball cleanly and managed what would probably have been a routine fly to center. But again, his hand, though still wrapped in a smaller bandage and with a padded batting glove, hurt a lot. He had not counted on that nor did he want to be a wuss about it.

Athletes play through pain, right? And it was just a small slice through the palm of his hand and only seven stitches. *Suck it up, Mack!* he thought. After letting two marginal pitches sail by, he swung again, connected, and sent a routine grounder toward short. This time, if anything, the pain was greater. Mack flung his bat at the screen next to the dugout, went to the bench, and sat down. And yes, he was pouting. Coach/Dad joined him for a moment.

"Hand hurt?"

"Was it that obvious?" His dad nodded. "I think maybe I could be a defensive replacement if you need one, but I can't bat."

"No problem. We'll work it out. I'll switch Larry over to short and give Andy a shot at second. You can help out by coaching the third-base side."

"Ah geez, Dad, I've never coached the bases and I'm not sure I even know the signs well enough."

"You're a smart kid. You'll be fine. Bunt is taking your hat off and putting it on. Steal is hands on hips. Hit-and-run is a tug on your right ear. A swipe across your chest takes off any signs given previously."

"We're not using a take sign anymore?"

"Nope. I've decided that all you guys know enough baseball to make your own decisions when it comes to swinging a bat or not."

So began Mack's baseball coaching career. He actually enjoyed working the signs, though a couple of times he forgot to look at his dad and missed passing along signs that might have mattered. It's hard to know, of course, since there is no guarantee that a steal or bunt or hit-and-run would have worked as planned. Nevertheless, the first time Mack came back to the dugout as the YJs took to the field and his dad quietly let him know that he had missed a sign, Mack promised he wouldn't let that happen again. And then, of course, he did. The second time, all his dad had to do was give one of his disappointed dad looks and Mack knew he had messed up. He mumbled, "Sorry," and made no promises, except to himself.

In retrospect, there was one other thing of note. In the coach's box, Mack felt almost as much a part of the game as he did playing shortstop. The signs were one thing. But he also had to make sure he was aware of the situation on the field at all times—how many outs, balls and strikes, runners on base, and whether they were leading off enough or too much, when infielders and the pitcher might be considering a pickoff move. His most important job as the third-base coach was verbal and nonverbal instructions to runners rounding second and third base after a hit and/or throw. Most of the time, the runner has his or her back to the play in the field and can't see what's going on. The third-base coach tells the runner to slide (both hands down), to stand at the bag or stop after rounding the bag (both hands up), or to keep on running (pinwheel motion).

The latter signals were crucial three different times during the game. In the top half of the third with Georgeena on first, Johnny Raymond doubled into right center. At first, Mack held Georgeena up at third (both hands up), but when the second baseman bobbled the cutoff throw, he sent her in to tie the score at three all. At the same time, he waved Johnny toward third and had him slide to beat the throw. Later in the seventh, with Larry Chen on second, Alan Alford singled sharply to left. Though it looked like the play would be close, Mack waved Larry around third and he scored when the catcher dropped the ball. Sigh of relief that time. He had been wrong, but it still turned out in favor of the YJs. Unfortunately, the final score went to the Callipa Bay Oysters, 8–7. It didn't quite fit, but Mack couldn't resist applying a sports news headline to his thoughts about the game: YJs shelled by Oysters. *Ha. Ha.*

*****

Mack hurried home after Thursday classes. He opted to skip the YJ's late-afternoon practice session. He told his dad he had work to do, which wasn't exactly the whole truth. It wasn't exactly a lie either.

Well, he wouldn't be himself if that didn't lead to some quiet philosophical reflection. *Someday,* he reflected, *I'm going to have to think through what it means to always tell the truth and when it is better (possibly) to tell a lie instead. For example, in the unlikely event that a girl runs down an alley right in front of me and then some guy with a baseball bat asks me which way she went, do I tell the truth or lie? Or slightly more likely, if somebody asks me if Johnny Raymond is queer, am I required to tell the truth? Or if I imply to my parents that I'm working at my real job, but really, I'm going to the park to practice something because if it doesn't work out and I tell a certain person what I'm doing, I'll hurt someone's feelings, is that a lie exactly?*

I've heard it said or written somewhere that telling the truth is always best because then, you won't have to worry about making something up to cover up your lie. And I have also heard that even if you tell a lie to avoid hurting someone's feelings when the truth wills out—as it always does—then no one will trust you again. So is telling the truth always the easy way? Sure didn't seem that way sometimes. Or was it the opposite? Sometimes lying seemed more the easy way out. Sometimes I wish doing the right thing was that simple.

Meanwhile, with a groan for his amateur philosophizing, he had grabbed his glove and a bag full of old baseballs and jogged to the park where hopefully a certain tennis court would not be in use. He was in luck. And there was the concrete wall he remembered at one end of the court. He had brought a large piece of chalk and crudely drew a home plate on the ground in front of the wall, a theoretical baseball strike zone and even a stick figure batter on one side directly on the wall. Then he marked off approximately sixty feet and drew another line. And for thirty minutes, he threw baseballs at the strike zone, gradually building up his velocity. For the next thirty minutes, he used his imagination to create a variety of game situations.

Three-two count. Fastball on the outside corner, drilled to left field for a base hit. Runner on first, put back foot on the pitching rubber and take the stretch. Look the runner back. Again with the stretch. Curveball—strike one. Two off-speed balls, both outside. Fastball catches the outside corner—two and two is the count. One throw over to first to hold the runner close (not really since there was no wall in that direction). Shake off the catcher's sign for another curveball. Fastball off the plate inside, but the batter swings and misses. Strike three. He's out a there.

Well, it was work of a sort. As he walked home after that first pitching workout, he was aware of several things. First, even with his injured hand, he could grip the ball adequately for most pitches. Second, he wasn't ready to take the mound for an actual game. His fastball might get him by for a couple of innings—if his control was good enough. Otherwise, he had no alternative pitch, breaking ball or changeup (he had even tried a knuckleball a few times) that he could count on. So no, he was not ready to tell his dad that he was suddenly an option for the team's pitching woes. However, trying to be objective here, he was also not hopeless. He needed practice and practice and practice—against a wall if that was all that was available. But maybe there was another option.

*****

When Mack looked out of the window of his room that Saturday morning, the overcast sky and drizzly rain gave him some hope that the late-afternoon game with the Black Knights would be canceled. He had taken a few practice swings with his favorite bat, and his hand was still bothering him. His dad would ask and he would tell him the truth: He still wasn't ready to play.

The rain stopped midmorning, and by noon, the sky was clear. There would be a ball game after all and likely another day in the third-base coaching box. *So be it.*

There are these kinds of days in every sport—a day when absolutely nothing goes right. In baseball, without accounting for the abilities of the opposing team, there are times when every hard-hit ball of your team goes straight to the glove of a defensive player or curves foul at the last second while every opposing team hit finds a hole in the defense, even short pop flies off the end of a bat. When your team is on defense, ground balls directly hit to infielders take awkward bounces off hidden rocks. Routine fly balls to the outfield are lost in the sun and land for triples. Umpires appear to have it in for you. Borderline pitches seem to be called strikes when your team is batting and balls when your pitcher is pitching.

Although it only *seemed* like all these things (and more) happened in the Yellow Jacket-Black Knight game that Saturday afternoon, enough did that nearly every player on the YJ bench was frustrated and discouraged. The one exception was Johnny Raymond who went three for four, stole two bases, and scored both YJ runs. The game did not actually start badly for the YJs. In his leadoff role, Johnny singled. Two outs later, he stole second. Alan Alford doubled him home with the first run of the game, but that was the YJ's last score until the ninth when Johnny doubled, stole third, and came home on a sac fly.

Otherwise, the YJ bats were silent. And poor pitching again didn't help. The Knights hadn't scored more than three runs in their first five games. Against YJ pitching, they scored nine.

As the team packed up and got ready to leave the field, Mack told his dad he would catch up with him later and jogged after Johnny. He had decided to act on an earlier inspiration—at least he thought it was an inspiration. Maybe if he had paused to think things through, he—*what*—*would have done nothing?*

As it was, when he caught up with Johnny near the exit to the park, he took a deep breath, but no words came. Had he thought this would be easy? Not really. Johnny said nothing either, but his look seemed to say, "What do you want?" Or that's how Mack read it.

"Great game, Johnny," he finally said. "I wish we could have given you more support." Johnny just stood there. *He sure isn't making this any easier*, he thought. "I have an idea. Listen, I know we kinda parted on the wrong foot the other night, and I do still want to be your friend. But this is also about baseball—my idea, I mean."

At least Johnny had stopped walking. He still didn't say anything much, but he did nod his head. "So?"

"So you know how except for today, there's not been much wrong with our offense but how our pitching basically sucks. No offense to Softy, but even he's not very sharp some days, and besides him, we've got about nothing."

"Go on. What's your idea?"

"Simple. You and I think I probably have the two best arms on the team. What if we were to do some regular pitching-and-catching workouts? Together, I mean. Then when we're ready, we tell my dad that he's got two other options. I was throwing balls against a wall at the tennis courts this week, but that's not really the same. We could use the team's catching equipment."

"You sure you want to be seen with me?"

"Look, I'm sorry that's the impression I left you with. The whole thing—"

"Meaning my sexual orientation."

"The whole thing—it just caught me by surprise. I didn't know what to say. But I've thought about little else since. And I'm clear. I would like to be your friend—not your lover but your friend. But even if you're not sure about that, this is also about baseball. So if you want it to be only about baseball, that's okay with me too. I think with a little work, you could be a good pitcher and you could sure help me with my pitching. That's what I'm asking. If you don't want to answer at this point, I get it. Let me know. Okay?"

Johnny said nothing—at first. Mack turned away, waved good-bye, and started to head down the street.

Johnny called after him, "I'll see you at the high school field tomorrow afternoon. They're playing against Wilson across town."

"Okay. Okay then."

CHAPTER 16

Prom

On Tuesday of prom week, the YJs suffered their third straight loss—this time to Charlie's Angels, 6–4. Mack had declared himself ready to play, though his hand was still sore and bandaged. He started out the game in the coaching box, but his dad put him in at shortstop in the fifth. He handled three ground balls, the last one a tough chance near the second-base bag, which he scooped up on the run and threw the hitter out by just a half step. On offense, he did not fare so well—a strikeout to end the sixth and a pop fly to first with runners on in the last of the eighth. Was he simply trying too hard? Was he unconsciously favoring his injured hand? Or was he in an average too much time off slump? Maybe he could convince Johnny to go to the Sportsplex batting cages after their scheduled Saturday pitching-catching practice.

Saturday was a bye date for the Yellow Jackets. Their next game would begin the second time through the schedule, starting again with the First Responders. The YJs had ended the first third of the season with a 3–3 record, which put them somewhere in the middle of the pack behind Charlie's Angels at 4–2 and the First Responders at 5–1.

Via text, Mack and Johnny had agreed to meet at the high school baseball field at 10:00 a.m. for their second individualized practice session. Wednesday's pitch/catch had been cut short by a thunderstorm moving through the area. That day, they had warmed up and Mack had taken a first turn pitching from the mound. Even that limited experience had reminded him how different it was to throw from a small hill as opposed to the flat surface near the tennis court. Johnny had been wise to suggest the high school field. They just had to make sure the high school team wasn't using it.

On Saturday, Mack grabbed a bag full of used baseballs, a catcher's mask and glove, a helmet, and a bat—in case they decided to include some batting practice. When he got to the field at 9:55 a.m., Johnny was already there firing a baseball at the backstop. Mack quickly put on his baseball spikes, grabbed the catcher's equipment, trotted over, and squatted behind home plate.

Fifteen minutes later, Mack was convinced that John Raymond was already the best pitcher on the YJ roster. True, he was a scrawny kid—by all appearances about six feet and 150 pounds—but he had a natural arm motion, reaching far beyond his back and somehow managing to put most of those 150 pounds behind a fastball that appeared to Mack to reach close to eighty-five miles per hour. This was definitely not the Johnny he had experienced in the one batting practice when he faced him as a hitter. That Johnny had thrown strikes and a decent breaking ball. But obviously, he had been holding something back. Mack held up a hand to forestall the next pitch.

"Hold on," he shouted, "I need to understand a couple of things, and besides, your fastball is hurting my catching hand. I need a break." He walked out to the mound, almost like a catcher might consult with a pitcher during a game. He thought briefly about throwing an arm around Johnny's shoulder in a friendly gesture but couldn't quite bring himself to that. Instead, he plunked the ball into Johnny's glove and shook his head.

"I can't believe what I'm seein'. Why haven't you been pitching all season? I knew you had a good arm—from center field. And I knew you could probably find the plate if you had to. And I knew I probably would have a rough time with your curveball if you could throw strikes with it. But this—you're ready for a college team right now, much less Lincoln High School. Unless, of course, I'm totally worthless as a baseball scout."

Johnny Raymond was quiet during and after Mack's brief speech—a shy, withdrawn response that was nearly the opposite of the flamboyant personality Mack had grown accustomed to. Johnny took a long hard look at the ground, scuffing a baseball shoe in front of the pitching rubber, digging a bit of a hole with the toe of his right shoe. He slowly turned his back and stared out toward center field—a few moments that felt like minutes to Mack. Then he returned his foot to the pitching rubber, took a full wind up, and fired the ball as hard as he could across home plate. The ball caromed off the backstop and rolled toward third base. It sounded like a shot.

"I was afraid of this," he muttered.

"Afraid of what?"

"Of this. I should have never let you talk me into this. You know things were just fine in my life until I got involved with you."

"Involved how? What? I don't understand."

"Well, not where your mind has obviously taken you. I didn't mean that." Mack continued with a puzzled look on his face. "You're messin' with me, man. What if I don't want to be a pitcher? What if I like my outfield life? What if I like playing center field for the Columbia City Sporting Goods Yellow Jackets?"

"Then stay in the outfield—if that's what you want."

"But that's not what you really think, not now. And this was never about two guys just hangin' out. If I want to stay in the baseball closet, that's my right."

"Look, Johnny, not everyone is out to game you. I told you what this was about for me—that I wanted to be your friend. But even if that wasn't possible, I thought that maybe we could really help the team. I meant both of those things, but hey, if you don't want to pitch, don't pitch. It's as simple as that."

"I don't believe you."

"I don't care what you believe or not. Actually, that's not true. That was the pissed-off me. I do care what you think and I care whether you believe me. I don't like it when people don't believe me when I'm speaking the truth. So I'll keep tryin'. The believing part is up to you. But unless you're going to take your ball and go home, it's my turn to throw. Here's the catcher's mitt."

*****

It was about five hours later. Mack awkwardly hooked the cummerbund around his waist, knotted his bow tie, and then stared into the full-length mirror. After the near debacle at the baseball field, he had changed and put in about three hours at the Spoon. Then it was a quick run to the tux rental place, then back home for another change before picking up Elana for their pre-prom dinner date. Not for the first time, he wondered why he was spending beaucoup bucks dressing himself in a fancy suit that made him uncomfortable, going to a classy restaurant that he would never go to on his own, and then attending a dance when he didn't especially like dancing and with a girl he had such mixed feelings about anyway.

He thought about Johnny denying that he had a gifted pitching arm—or whatever he was denying. *Maybe I'm not so different. Here I am with my own "gifts": an attractive girlfriend, enough money to waste on a big night on the town in a fancy suit like this thing. Hey, maybe I'm just as bad at believing in myself as a baseball player. It hasn't been much of a season thus far. And maybe he's right. Why should I try to convince a guy that he's good? Doesn't he have to do that himself?*

With one last-moment preparatory stare, Mack readied himself to walk downstairs for mom inspection and the probable "Oh, isn't he handsome, Karl?" Mack wasn't disappointed, though he tried to smile and not smirk. And Karl nodded his approval. Well, that's how Mack took his dad's nod. "If you have time, bring that girl by so we can take pictures," said his mom as he headed out the door.

Picking up Elana involved other rituals, most of which he didn't get. What's with moms and photos? Elana's mom had to pose both of them several times. Her father took a moment from the TV show he was watching to poke his head into the living room. Was that a glare? He apparently had nothing to say. Elana's sisters—the California one was visiting for a couple of weeks—clustered around in semi admiration of her dress but more to do their own glaring. Or was it just checking him out for acceptability? Whatever. On the surface, some of it was pretty ordinary stuff, but something about it was uncomfortable to Mack. And for the first time, he could better understand Elana's need to exit her home premises as quickly as possible.

In the fifteen-minute drive to McCormick's Beachside Restaurant, Elana did most of the talking. Mack listened with half a brain and thought about baseball and Johnny Raymond with the other half. At least he thought he was listening with that first half.

"Mack. Mack. FRANCIS McKYER. Where in the hell did you disappear to? You aren't listening to me—that's for sure!"

"Sure, I am. Go on."

"No, you can't get away with that. What was I talking about?"

"Uh, chemistry? English? Girlfriends' gossip? Oh, all right, you caught me. What were we talking about?"

"Oh no, you don't. If you aren't going to listen, why should I waste my breath?"

"Speaking of breaths, can we take one and start over?"

Elana obviously thought that over for a few moments of silence before saying, "I guess."

"So what did I miss?"

"I was mostly just saying what an a——hole my stepdad was."

"Stepdad? You mean you were talking about your family for once. I don't believe it." She glared, looking for a moment rather like her stepfather.

"He could have at least said hi or shook your hand or something. And the rest of the family wasn't much better. My mom traipsing about like she's some kind of professional photographer—not saying much of anything except 'Smile,' and 'Don't be home too late.' Ha! Ha! As if she really cared. And Becky acting like she was ready to take a bite out of you. At least now you maybe understand why I hate them all."

"They weren't that bad, Elana. Maybe they're feeling anxious about impressing your new boyfriend."

"So now you think you're my first boyfriend or something."

And this was said simultaneously by Mack, "That's not what I said."

"You just don't get it, Mr. Everything Is All Right in His Family World. Well, it's not in mine."

Outside, it was a pleasant evening. The sun was setting somewhere beyond the western mountains, and there was a soft, yellow-orange glow on the water as they drove into the restaurant parking lot. They had arrived—perhaps not a moment too soon. Mack jumped out of the car first and caught Elana gently by the arm before she could stomp off toward the entrance.

"Hold on a minute. Please. I'm sorry. I apologize for not listening to you. I apologize for not understanding what things are like in your family. And I'm sorry that I tried to make it better by teasing you about the boyfriend stuff."

She stopped trying to pull away from him and leaned her head against his shoulder. "I'm sorry too. I shouldn't let that stuff bother me anymore. It never changes."

Mack cupped her chin with his hand and kissed her gently on the lips. "All right then. Agreed? We forget family for a while and have a good time, starting with a meal at a fine restaurant—at least that's what my forty closest Instagram friends tell me. But I hasten to add NOT my family."

They both laughed. "Not my family either."

And that might have been the start of the recovery from dreadful date and the ushering in of perfect junior prom date. Unfortunately, the world often doesn't unfold the way we would like or plan. But for the moment, all was well.

As they were escorted by the hostess to their window-side table overlooking the sea and the sunset, Mack and Elana saw and greeted several couples they knew from school. There was Lamont with Erica, Kerry with Georgia, and Tad with Katy among others. It was almost like a fancy, more subdued version of the high school cafeteria. And of course, the prices on the menu were quite a bit higher than cafeteria fare.

It was, by universal agreement, a good meal. Mack only had a brief (and silent) bit of remorse when he saw the final bill. It would have paid for a lot of snacks at the Spoon or perhaps professional tennis and golf lessons for both of them. But hey, you only go to one high school junior prom in your life.

With some mixed feelings, on Mack's part, they skipped dessert and went for a brief walk along the beach boardwalk. Elana had said that she didn't want to be among the first to arrive at the prom and Mack certainly didn't care, though he was not about to say so. The dance was scheduled to begin at 8:00 p.m. The time was only 7:45 p.m., and they had less than a twenty-minute drive. So for a while, they walked and talked but not about family or school or baseball. It is a big world out there, a lot to try and understand. They were almost adults and knew perhaps less than they thought they knew. Still, it was a small but fine thing to be with someone who tried to listen—at least for that moment. *Maybe this will be an okay evening after all.*

At 8:45 p.m., they walked into a transformed Lincoln High cafeteria hand in hand. Their divided agendas clashed briefly when Mack tried to make a beeline to the dessert bar and Elana to the dance floor. She won. It was about a half hour later before Mack got her to agree to take a break. He had been to dances before, but *believe it or not*, he had not actually brought a date to a dance. Usually, he had wandered around, talking to other singles, occasionally dancing when coerced or teased into it, trying to feel natural and sophisticated but knowing he wasn't pulling it off. Girls had rarely been interested in another dance after his first fumbling efforts.

So Mack wasn't expecting to actually enjoy the dancing, but he did enjoy watching Elana. He quickly discovered that what he feared was actually the case—i.e., the movements of the dances that seemed to come naturally to Elana and most of the other girls he observed, didn't for him. He felt as awkward as he imagined most girls would feel on a football field. It was one thing to dance in a crowded family room like the New Year's Eve party and quite another to be out there on a large floor with a lot of space for everyone to see how really bad of a dancer you were. Eventually, Mack discovered that if he copied Elana's moves, then it at least seemed like they were somewhat together. Of course, this was all with respect to the beat of the rock-and-roll songs that formed most of the band's repertoire. When the band surprised him with a slower-tempo waltz, it seemed like the idea was more about melting into Elana's arms than it was any kind of coordinated movement. But hey, that wasn't so bad.

For better than half the evening, the two of them established a kind of rhythm. They were on the dance floor for a longer time than Mack thought possible. Then they would take a break and try to hold a conversation with a few friends. Unless the band was also breaking, talk was difficult because of the noise level of much of the music. Still, they managed. Mack got his dessert, and they both drank about five cups of punch. It was well after 10:30 p.m. And during one of the band breaks, Mack and Elana were sitting with Tad and Katy as well as Kerry and his date, when Mack spotted Johnny Raymond, apparently on his way toward the boy's restroom. He hadn't noticed Johnny before, but he had seen a couple of the guys that appeared to be following him toward the facilities—Darrel Coffin and Mark Wenger.

Coffin and Wenger were known at Lincoln as guys you didn't want to mess with. In short, they were oftentimes quietly referred to as bullies. Reputations can develop unfairly, and Mack had never had occasion to experience the kind of behavior they were known for. But suddenly, he felt a strong need to make use of the boy's room himself. Briefly, he thought about asking Tad or Kerry or both to join him, but that's the kind of thing girls do, right? It was probably nothing. He'd be fine. Johnny would be fine.

Once he had made up his mind, Mack excused himself and walked, rather quicker than he might have, out of the cafeteria and down the hall to the restroom area. He paused outside the door where a weaselly looking guy he didn't know was standing, leaning against the wall. The noise of the band reforming made it impossible to hear anything going on beyond the door.

But when Mack started to walk through, the weasel guy stepped in front of him and said, "I wouldn't go in there now if I were you."

Mack looked him in the eye and asked, "Are you serious? When a guy's got to go, a guy's got to go."

"Yeah."

And he backed up, quickly stuck his head in the door, and yelled a couple of names. Before he could think much more about it, Mack shoved his way past weasel face and moved to the side of the door so he couldn't be blindsided. The scene that confronted him was chaotic. There were a couple of guys standing near the door as if to block further access to the area. Otherwise, they were not doing much of anything. But all eyes focused down the row of toilet stalls. There, Mack could see the rear ends of two unidentifiable guys doing something that was taking all their concentration. The first two guys tried to grab and detain Mack while yelling, "Warren, what the hell? You weren't supposed to let anybody in."

But at that point, though he hadn't seen Johnny yet, Mack had seen enough to know he either had to bust back out of the space or do something where he was. He threw a couple of basketball-rebound-clearing elbows into the guts of the two trying to hold him and raced toward the last toilet stall.

He had found Johnny. Not surprisingly, the two backsides he had seen belonged to Wenger and Coffin. They were both holding Johnny over the toilet bowl and attempting to push his head into the water. Johnny was kicking back at whatever his feet could reach.

"Goddamn it, faggot. Hold still or it'll just get worse!" yelled one of the two.

"Sit on his legs, Mark. I'll take his neck."

"Oh, just piss on him." That was about all they managed to get out before Mack acted. He grabbed the first guy he could. It turned out to be Coffin.

"Let him go. Now. And I won't report you."

Coffin tried to free a hand to throw a punch at Mack while saying, "Oh, Johnny, Johnny Rainbow, your big-star athlete lover is here."

"Here for his own special shit-dipping ceremony, huh," said Wenger, also turning around, which gave Johnny a chance to pull away from them.

While they faced Mack and their backs were turned, Johnny climbed onto the toilet seat. Mack found his elbows useful again, throwing one into Coffin's midsection. At the same time, he hit

Wenger with a left-handed jab to the gut. Wenger returned a punch, which caught Mack near his left eye. At the same time, Johnny jumped on Coffin's back, forcing him to fall facedown on the hard concrete floor. Wenger was backing up trying to throw another punch or two, but it was apparent he wasn't that interested in fighting back on his own. The other three guys had already left. He followed.

"Come on, Johnny. Let's get out of here," yelled Mack.

That might have worked to save them the trouble that would follow, but Johnny hung around long enough to give Coffin a hard boot to the belly while the bully was just managing to sit up. Coffin groaned and sank back to the floor. Johnny did not look good either. His hair was covered with toilet water, which dripped down his face. His tux was rumpled and torn in a couple of places. And he was limping on one leg. Unfortunately, when Mack finally got his attention and was trying to steer him away from the space and from Darrel Coffin, in the boy's room door came Mack's homeroom and history teacher, Mr. Fletcher, and another man Mack didn't know.

Mack and Johnny stopped where they were. There was no denying that they were part of whatever had gone on. The man Mack didn't know walked over to Coffin to check on him. Although he couldn't hear the words, from Mack's perspective, far too much concern was being expressed.

Coffin stared at him and Johnny, then said all too clearly, "They started it, Mr. Ames. I was, ya know, doin' my business when that guy"—he pointed at Johnny—"gave me a shove for no reason. Naturally, I pushed him back and I guess he slipped, fell in to one of the toilets, and got himself a little wet."

Mack's jaw must have dropped several inches. Johnny was not as speechless.

"He's lying. It was all him and his henchmen—Wenger, Holmes, and Weasel-face Warren."

The two teacher types glanced at one another. Ames took charge.

"Darrel, can you walk on your own?" Coffin made a bit of a production pulling himself to his feet. For a moment, Mack wondered if he was really hurt, but when the teachers weren't looking at him, Coffin flashed a smirky smile at Mack and Johnny.

He didn't have to say, "I'm fine. Those two don't got what it takes to bring me down. If they hadn't jumped me from behind, you'd be taking them to the hospital."

"All right then," said Ames. "You boys here by yourselves?"

To that, he got three different answers, one a great surprise to Mack. Johnny said one word, "Yes."

Mack, of course, said he was "Here with my girlfriend."

Coffin waited and added, "I'm here with my girlfriend, too, Elana lots of lovin'."

"You bastard," cursed Mack and started to put his hands back into fighting position. He quickly took a deep breath and calmed himself before either teacher needed to interfere, then said clearly, "He is not with Elana. She is with me." Coffin just grinned.

"Well, that ought to be easy enough to sort out," Ames countered. "Mr. Fletcher, you take McKyer and I'll manage Coffin. The dance is over for you three. Since you're on your own, Raymond, you can be the first to leave. I'll expect you in my office first thing Monday morning." Johnny shrugged his shoulders, glanced sympathetically toward Mack, and left.

Ames and Fletcher marched the other two boys back into the dance area. Wenger and the other boy's room bystanders were nowhere in sight. Before Mack had a chance, Coffin pointed out the table where Elana and the others still lingered.

Coffin broke away from Ames and put his arm around Elana's shoulders, saying, "I guess we're going to have to leave the dance, sweetheart. The football hero just picked a fight with me." Elana had the good grace to look stunned and for a moment, speechless.

"So you are with this guy?" said Ames, gesturing toward Coffin.

"Uh, no. Actually, I'm with the football hero."

Coffin managed to look deeply hurt. "Why, Elana? How could you throw me over for this piece of—" His words tailed off as though he had suddenly realized that swearing in front of teachers wouldn't fit the persona he was attempting to portray. "I guess if that's the way you are, then I should've dropped you last week." He smiled again with the same smirk, which belied his words to the teachers, "That's just the way women are, I guess. You think you can count on them to be faithful and they mess around behind your back." He shook his head several times as though he simply couldn't believe this incredible turn of events.

Fletcher stepped in at that point and said to Elana, "So you <u>are</u> with Mack. Is that right?"

She nodded but added, "Right now, I don't know as I want to be with either one of them."

Ames took charge again. "I certainly can see why that would be the case. But for now, you are to go home with whoever brought you here—right now. No chatting up with your friends—either of you." He glanced first at Mack and then around the table as though to memorize the other faces. "Elana, I may want to see you again on Monday after I've talked to the combatants. McKyer, take the young woman home. I'll see you in my office first thing Monday morning as well—you or Raymond, whoever gets there first. Coffin, you can hang out with me and Mr. Fletcher for a few more minutes. Let's the three of us take a walk to my office."

Mack was more than stunned. He wanted to stay and tell everyone what had really happened. He knew everyone at that table would believe him. He wasn't so sure about Elana. Oh, she would believe him, but she would also be super angry. He had, after all, ruined their big date. And as much as he knew it hadn't been his fault, convincing her might not be so easy. They grabbed their belongings and left.

Mack was determined to stay quiet until they were in the privacy of his car. He had forgotten about Coffin's henchmen. There they were, five of them (including Wenger), behind the gym—leaning against the wall, talking, and smoking cigarettes. Unfortunately, they were also in a direct line from the school door to the area where Mack had parked. And they weren't in a quiet mood.

"Lover boy."

"Gay lover."

"Homo. Homo."

Those were said along with a wolf whistle. Was that for Elana or for him? And did it matter? Elana swerved as though she had some form of violence on her mind. Mack caught her by the sleeve and said, "No, it won't do any good. That's just the way they are. And one fight a night is plenty for me."

She took his arm as they crossed quickly to their ride. "You better have a way of making me understand this," she said as they slammed the car doors, shutting out the background chant of "Johnny Rainbow. Johnny Rainbow."

The ride back to Elana's place was mostly a quiet one. Mack knew he had to say something, but he couldn't think of the right words. He had not been at all sure how he had wanted this date to end all the way back to when he had first asked her to go with him. Then more recently, the whole hiking-trip thing had stirred up a bunch of feelings. This night's down-and-up pre and post dinnertime and the dance-floor turn-ons had been unsettling to say the least. Finally, of course, he was reliving the scene in the boy's room. What should he have done differently?

Mack pulled up to a darkened spot a few houses down the street from Elana's. He messed with the radio until he found some softer-mood music, then turned and looked Elana full in the face and said, "Well?"

"Well, what?"

"I'm sorry. I didn't mean for the evening to end like this."

"You didn't? Are you sure?"

Mack was quiet for a moment. Was he sure? Had he somehow stirred up a situation that would help him avoid dealing with his feelings toward Elana?

"Do you want to know what happened?"

It was Elana's turn to stay quiet for a bit and then finally say, "Yeah. Okay. Truth now."

So he told her as best he remembered from the moment he had followed the other boys to the restroom.

"Let me see your eye," she said and turned his head back toward her. "It's starting to change color," she added, then kissed him lightly on the lips. "Does it hurt?"

He nodded, "A little."

"You should probably go home and put some ice on it."

This was not, he realized, what he wanted to hear. "That can wait a bit. I want to know what you're thinking."

"I don't know what to think, Mack." Then she added, "Sometimes—like up at the lake or after dinner tonight or on the dance floor—I think you really like me. But then there's what happens every time we get close or so it seems. We start to, you know, like express our feelings. Then you almost bleed to death. Then I don't hear from you for days. It seems like something always happens and you disappear and…and don't tell me why. Now don't get me wrong. I'm not antigay or anything. But what am I supposed to make of this? We're having a fine evening, then you disappear again, and the next thing I know is you've been in a fight protecting this gay friend of yours. Are…are you gay, Mack? 'Cause if you are, that's okay. I mean I'll understand. And we'll just, you know, be friends or such. And I'll, you know, like get on with my life—"

The more Elana said, the more Mack felt his anger bubbling to the surface. *Damn it. Doesn't anyone understand this—understand me?* Elana was in midsentence when Mack, forgetting his seat belt was still fastened and his face bruised, awkwardly reached for her and pulled her toward him in an almost-crushing embrace.

After kissing her rather thoroughly, he pulled back and said, "Now is that the kiss of a gay man?"

"I guess not," she offered, "but I don't want to be your experimental straight chick either."

"If that's what you think," he started.

But quite suddenly, the whole night got to him: the ups and downs with Elana, the bullying of Johnny, the fight, his aching head, the pending visit to the principal's office, the general meanness and cruelty of the world. And though thoroughly chagrinned, Mack began to cry. And once he had started, he couldn't stop for a good five minutes. He felt Elana's hand stroking his arm, but at the moment, he really didn't want her comfort either. As embarrassing as it was to admit even to himself, he wanted his mom or even his dad to hold him like he was still maybe six years old.

Oh geez, he thought, *now she's really going to think I'm gay. But what is, is what is.* And for this time and place, he wondered if there was anything to salvage here—his relationship to Elana, his reputation, maybe even his future at Lincoln High School. "You're right," he said, "I've got to go home and put some ice on my eye." He brushed away her hand, started the car, and drove the short distance to the front of Elana's house. They said, "Good night." They didn't touch again.

CHAPTER 17

Unfair

The last couple of weeks before summer vacation break are usually low anxiety for most high school students—except for one or two final exams or maybe a paper that was put off until the last minute. Teachers, generally speaking, tend to realize that they have crammed about as much into the heads of their students as is possible in one year. Classrooms become more relaxed and informal. The wiser teachers keep you busy but with interesting stuff that might actually apply to your life. Extracurricular activities dominate the scene: end-of-the-year concerts, the last major theatrical production, last meetings of school-related organizations, and of course, conference tournaments or meets in the spring sports: track, tennis, golf, etc., and baseball. And of course, there is the distribution of the high school annual (at Lincoln High entitled the Lincoln Log). And there are all the goodbyes, exchanged wishes for a fun summer, and on a final, more serious note, a fond (well, maybe not always fond) farewell to all the graduating seniors.

That's how it's supposed to be, thought Mack as he made his way down the sidewalks, up the stairs, and down the hall toward the principal's office early Monday morning on the last week of school. He was determined to get things over with as soon as possible so he could get to homeroom on time, no further questions asked, thank you very much. As far as he could see, he was the first student in the building. But after sitting in the waiting area outside the office by himself for fifteen minutes, he began to wish he hadn't been so early.

Finally, the receptionist told him he could go on in. However, as he started to go toward Principal Grandy's office, she stopped him and pointed toward another office space around the corner and further down the hall, saying, "You're seeing Vice Principal Ames. His name is on the door."

Mack had been nervous enough—now that doubled. He was used to Principal Grandy. He basically liked him, even though their last meeting hadn't exactly been fun. But Ames. If Saturday night had been any kind of a test, Mack knew he had failed. For whatever reason, though they hadn't met before, he had gotten the clear impression that Ames hadn't liked him at all. Before the prom, he hadn't even known who Ames was or that Lincoln had recently hired a new vice principal. He didn't exactly like the implications of the title. But *here we go.* No more diddling around. What is, is. Mack knocked on the office door.

"Come in. Take a seat, McKyer. I'll be with you in a moment." Mack took a seat across the desk from the vice principal. His chair seemed a bit low to the floor or maybe it was Ames's desk chair that was heightened. In any case, he felt like he was gazing up toward the stern countenance of a court judge. Perhaps that's the impression that Ames wanted to give. Or maybe Mack's imagination was ruling the moment. For a couple of minutes, Ames continued to attend to some messages on his computer. Finally, he hit the send button, shut down whatever he was working on, and turned back to Mack.

"So, McKyer, have you given any further thought to your role in Saturday night's episode? Mack nodded. "If so, I'd like to hear what you have to say for yourself before I let you know what I have decided as a disciplinary measure."

Mack took a deep breath. "Well, sir," he said, "I was sitting at a table with my date when I saw Johnny headed toward the men's room followed by Coffin and Wenger—"

Ames interrupted, "I'm not interested in a rehashing of the whole story. I have a good handle on that. Just tell me about your unfortunate choices."

"That's not fair, Mr. Ames. It wasn't a matter of choices. Something just didn't look right and I—"

Ames interrupted again, "Of course, it was a matter of choices, McKyer. But we'll get to that in a moment. I'm giving you a chance to defend your choice."

"Okay. I decided to follow the others toward the restroom without knowing what I would find. At first there was a guy standing at the door who didn't want to let me in."

"Yes, I know. So then you forced your way in like a fullback hitting a hole in the line. Is that right?"

"Not exactly. I just knew that Johnny was in trouble and I needed to help him out."

"It didn't occur to you to immediately find a teacher or other chaperone to do their job."

"There wasn't time. Everything happened so fast. Once inside I could see—"

"That's enough. I know what happened next. You shoved your way in in this rescue attempt and ended up creating a much bigger problem where people could have been hurt much more seriously. Isn't that right?"

"No, it's not right. They were bullying Johnny, trying to—"

"I said that's enough, McKyer. From my point of view, you made a bad situation much worse. I know you big-time athletes enjoy playing heroic roles, but in times like this, you over reach and people like your friend Raymond and boys like Coffin pay the price of too much muscle and too little brain. By the way, Mr. Coffin's mother called in this morning. His injuries are so bad that he won't be able to attend school for the rest of the year. The potential of a law suit is there."

Mack lapsed into stunned silence. He could not believe what he was hearing. It was such an unfair interpretation of events. Ames obviously didn't want to listen to him, not really, so he tuned Ames out as well. He sat there, watching lips move but hearing only mumbles of sound until he caught a last piece.

"You're a football player, aren't you, McKyer?" Mack nodded. "Since it's so near the end of the school year, it doesn't make much sense to expel you for a day or two. These last few days are always such a waste anyway. What would you miss? So I've decided that the most teachable thing we can do with you is to keep you out of football for a while. You'll miss the first two games of the next season. At which time, we'll revisit your case. If you appear to have learned your lesson, you can rejoin the team. Otherwise, another decision will be made at that time. I shall inform Mr. Smitson of your situation. You may go." And he turned his back to supposedly attend to some papers that needed filing. For a moment, Mack sat unmoving. He could not believe what he had heard.

"But, Mr. Ames, we played for the city championship this year, and there's a good chance we'll be equally good next fall. And I was the starting quarterback. Doesn't—"

"That'll be all, Mr. McKyer. Maybe you should have thought of that before crashing into that boy's room and throwing your weight around.

"But don't you—"

"If you hurry, you may make second bell."

CHAPTER 18

Unbelievable

As Mack stumbled out of the VP's office, he barely gave a nod to Johnny Raymond who was sitting close by, awaiting his turn. Mack shook his head in a nonverbal warning to what Johnny might be facing, then made his way down the hall as the bell rang, telling him he would be late to homeroom. His mind raced back to the familiar emotions of that day back in late March when he had to decide what to do when he did not see his name on the baseball team roster. The temptation was to do something close to what he had done then—run, escape, hide, get away to a place where he would not have to deal with anything. It was so unfair. He wanted to scream—literally. But that and most of his other choices would likely end with another seat in the principal's or vice principal's office. So he would master his tears and his anger this time—he had to. But how?

Mr. Fletcher was talking to the class when Mack slipped through the door and made his way around the back of the room and down to his seat on the third row right behind Katy Saunders. To Mack's relief, Fletcher ignored him and continued with his report on, of all things, the new administrative policies regarding school bullying. Considering his frame of mind, that was probably the only topic that could have grabbed Mack's attention. And it did. He listened to one suggestion in particular: Students were mandated to report any bullying to a schoolteacher or administrator as soon as possible *and* they were not to attempt to stop the bullying themselves. *Why not?*

his inner voice screamed. *What if there's not enough time and some-one's well-being is in jeopardy? Are we supposed to wait until someone is murdered?*

The bell rang again, and everyone began to move toward their first regular class. A couple of students, notably Katy, managed to ask him how he was doing.

"Not well," he squeaked out, "but now's not the time or place. Catch ya later."

Before he could make it out of the classroom, however, Fletcher stopped him and asked for a moment, saying, "Mack, do you have a few minutes after your last class today?"

What could he say? "Sure."

"See you at three ten then."

"Here?"

"Here."

*****

Mack made it through the rest of the school day on automatic pilot. With his swollen eye and the reports that had already circulated since Saturday night, he could hardly hide that he was upset from his friends. Though it was undoubtedly too late, he did not, however, want to add more fuel to the school gossip. His standard response to most folks had been "Yeah, I'm okay, but I don't want to talk about it right now."

When Mack entered Fletcher's classroom after the closing bell, he went armed with a good excuse to keep things short. He was due at the Spoon less than a half hour later.

Mack had always liked Mr. Fletcher both as his homeroom teacher and in his American history class. Fletcher was good at mak-ing history come alive and relevant to the current times. But mostly, at least in Mack's experience, Fletcher had always seemed like a good guy, a person who genuinely cared about his students. However, this situation was different and Mack really did not know what to expect.

"Have a seat, Mack," said the teacher and then he grabbed another chair a few feet away on the same level. *Unlike Ames,* Mack reflected, *who had maintained his distance behind a desk.* "I mostly wanted to see how you are doing and express my concern about things turning out as they have."

"Then you know about my time with Mr. Ames." Fletcher nodded. "I'm sorry," Mack added, "but I really don't get it. Was I supposed to just let Coffin and Wenger drowned Johnny in the toilet? I tried, but they were not about to listen to reason."

"I get it," responded Fletcher, "but that is not how Mr. Ames sees it. And in this, he gets the final say."

Mack took a deep breath and felt himself shiver with the realization that his barely buried hopes here were gone. "So there's nothing you can do?"

"I can imagine how difficult this is for you, Mack. But I'm still going to ask you to think about things from Mr. Ames point of view. He's new here, and he's been given a tough job."

"With all due respect, Mr. Fletcher, I don't give a rip about how tough a job he has. He's supposed to be the adult in this situation. He's got to know about Coffin and Wenger's reputations. I may have rushed in a little too quickly, but I don't think so. He's got no right to blame me for 95 percent of what went down."

"Mack, Mack, that's not the point. I know you much better than he does. But his job is to be as fair and unbiased as he can be, which means to treat each of you according to what he saw and heard—not based on my opinion or yours that you are the good guy here. And the facts he had to deal with were several boys claiming that you were the aggressor, hearing from the girl in question that she didn't especially want to keep company with either one of you, and seeing Coffin laid out on the floor barely able to get up on his own and later staying home from school this week because of a doctor's orders. And what he apparently hears from you is a denial that anything was your fault and the defense that you should be excused because you're a football star."

"But that's not what I said. And I'm afraid you're not going to like this part at all, but if I were faced with the same situation, I would do what I did all over again!" With that, Mack got up to go. He was done. There clearly was no way he was going to influence anyone in authority to step in and change what had now been ordered.

"Wait a second, Mack, please. I do want you to know that I believe you. I wish you had made a different choice, but I do believe you."

"But you have no power to change anything, right?"

"That is true for the reasons I shared with you. Mr. Ames is doing what he thinks is best for Lincoln High School and I need to support him in that."

"Mr. Fletcher, that's not right." And he left.

*****

The calls and texts started coming in almost immediately. The texts ranged from expressions of concern for Mack's well-being, questions about what he was going to do about it, and even a couple of insults or threats from anonymous sources—as in "You better be paying someone to watch your back," or "Never thought you were the one to lead our team anyway." Mack ignored them all. And slowly but with increased intensity, he felt his anger begin to build beyond any he remembered feeling at any other time in his life. It was the unbelievable *unfairness* of it all. If he had been a different kind of kid, he might very well have figured out where Ames lived and bought about five dozen eggs.

He expressed a piece of it to Randal during one of his Spoon work breaks, mostly so he'd understand if Mack went off on one of the customers. Sometimes he did feel like throwing a scoop of ice cream at someone, demanding extra attention when they were in one of their busier times or chasing another person down with a mop in hand after they appeared to intentionally mess up their booth seats or left a pile of garbage underneath a table. Randal nodded and invited him to stay after closing if he wanted. Mack did know he needed to talk to someone and particularly someone not directly involved with Lincoln High School, but it would be late so he asked for a rain check. He needed to get home.

And parents? Yes. Mack wanted them to know everything and nothing at the same time. He wanted them to be his safety net and to work this thing through on his own. He had run by the basics of the prom events Sunday—the day after. With his eye, there was little sense in hiding the fight part. They knew about the expected meeting with the principal but not the result. Their texts were among those ignored. They were waiting up for him when he got off work.

The parent meeting actually went better than expected. His mom wanted to come up with a solution and then have a face-to-face with Ames who would, she thought, be convinced by reason. Mack was surprised by his dad's anger. Before Mack could talk him down, Karl McKyer was ready to march down to the school in the morning and give the vice principal a literal piece of his mind.

"Thanks, but no thanks," Mack said. "I mean I'm glad I have parents who got my back. Probably a lot wouldn't have that. And I appreciate it. But given this situation and the players involved, I think you'd just make things worse. It was clear to me from the first that Ames was not going to change his mind. And the more I tried to explain things, the less he was willing to listen. Oh, he probably wouldn't interrupt you as much. Maybe he would listen more, but when it comes down to it, he would think you were supporting me because I'm your kid—not because I was in the right. And I don't like it, but he's convinced himself that he's right and I don't think he is the kind of person that easily gets to the I've-made-a-mistake place. Promise me you won't try to reason with him."

They had reluctantly agreed. Mack said, "Good night," and went upstairs to his bed. He lay there for a good two hours, but sleep would not come. He was angry. He was justified. He was a damn fool over and over again. Starting with—well—at least as far back as the semi date with Lisa, Johnny "Rainbow" Raymond, the semi date with Katy, the day hike with Elana, the hand injury, the ER, Elana, the prom, Johnny, the fight, Elana, Ames, and now. All of it cycling through his head over and over again.

On Tuesday morning, he rolled out of bed with the alarm sounding and groaned. When had he finally managed to fall asleep? His head hurt. His hand hurt. When had he managed to bang it up again? *Oh yeah, probably the fight,* he thought. He could barely see out of his eye and felt a stab of fear that maybe he was going blind on one side. He coughed. He took a deep breath and coughed again. He suppressed it, blew his nose, and coughed again. *No,* he thought, *I will not be a child and avoid facing my problems again.* He showered, dressed, and walked downstairs to the kitchen.

His mom took one look at him and said, "You don't look good. I think maybe you're coming down with something." She felt his forehead. "Can't tell. I'm going to get the thermometer." Mack tried to tell her he was fine, but truth of the matter was he was not fine and he was grateful for an excuse—a good one this time—to stay home.

That meant missing the Yellow Jackets game, a return match with the First Responders. But another truth be told, he really didn't want to play baseball. And that told him something. Usually, missing a game where he knew his teammates would be counting on him was the last thing he would do if at all possible. Not this time. He didn't want to play. He didn't want to be counted on. He didn't want to interact with Johnny Raymond or explain his black eye to anyone. School was bad enough—had been bad enough on Monday. For once, Mack agreed with his parents: If he wasn't well enough to go to school, then he wasn't well enough to play ball. So be it.

CHAPTER 19

Provisional Goodbyes

Of course, nothing is ever so simple. Could he milk this illness for the rest of the school year as apparently Darrel Coffin was doing? So now he was in a different kind of fight. And he recognized it for what it was—essentially face things straight on or run away from them. First and foremost among those things? His frame of mind. He searched within for a word and finally came up with *depressed.* Other words fit too—like *powerlessness, rage, hurt, feeling sorry for self.* But he guessed *depressed* captured his overall mood as well as anything. And the thing about depression? It leads to or shadows over so much else and turns all of life that it touches into a wasteland. The most appealing thing for Mack at the moment was a desire to sleep and forget everything. And that's what he knew he needed to fight—after he actually did go back to bed and sleep for ten hours.

About four in the afternoon, he woke up long enough to check the time. He thought about jumping up and throwing on his baseball uniform, sneaking out of the house, and peddling his bike to the game. But that is one of the problems when your dad is the coach. Mack knew he would not exactly be welcomed with open arms. More than likely he'd have been told to turn around and go back home. Wisely but without much thought, he turned over and slept for another hour. At 6:00 p.m., he showered, dressed, and went downstairs where he would have announced to everyone that he was well recovered, but clearly, no one was home. They had all gone to the game. He was therefore depressed, lonely, and hungry, which meant that at least he did not want to starve himself to death. He decided he couldn't wait for the late dinnertime of the rest of the family. Eggs, toast, and leftover fruit salad—with slightly browned and squishy bananas—were easy enough to throw together.

Mack was digging into a semi-stale brownie à la mode when his mom and Jana made it back with a large pizza and a side of chicken soup, the latter obviously for him. He immediately declared himself better and not in the need of chicken soup, though he did grab a piece of pizza. News of another Yellow Jacket loss did not help his mood, but next to his long list of other problems, it didn't seem like much of a deal. When his dad arrived a few minutes later, he tried to be appropriately consoling, but his heart couldn't quite go there. *It was just a small-time commercial league baseball game. Hopes that they would win their league championship and take on the high school team and that he would have the chance to somehow redeem himself now seemed quite unrealistic. That's all.*

The immediate issue of facing his high school community loomed. He had managed a day off, if that's what it was, but he had made up his mind. Even if he didn't feel that great, Mack was determined. He would be back in school for the next three days if it killed him.

After another restless night—Mack figured he'd still slept about sixteen of the last twenty-four hours—he rolled out of bed and made it through his morning routine, which included a lengthy time looking into a mirror at his still-swollen eye. Was it his imagination or had the eye changed color again during the night? Was it less yellow and even more black? Was he being stupid when he could spend the day watching TV and being generally pampered? "Face it," Mack, he said to his bruised face, "there are some things you can change and some you can't." To make sure he wasn't looking for a reprieve during breakfast, Mack snuck his way to the downstairs freezer, grabbed a handful of ice, and ran it around his neck and over his face. "That should help," he added before enduring a last-minute temperature check from his mom.

While she was considering the results, Mack headed out the door. Behind came a motherly semi shout, "Are you sure you're okay? The thermometer reads 97.1. How can that be?" He turned and waved. No words seemed necessary. Maybe he was not exactly totally himself yet, but he was walking upright and at least up to pretending that everything was okay again.

If it weren't for the still-throbbing headache and the gradually increasing sight impairment, that first day back was better than Mack's expectations. Of course, some of that had to do with these being the last days of school before the summer break. There was no homework to speak of, no tests to stress over, and lots of time to do little more than hang out with friends. And wonder of wonders, based on conversations with some of those friends and the general spirit of the nods, smiles, and greetings from the wider public, he was at least a welcome person of interest for these waning days of the school year.

It quickly became obvious that the prom story had spread. Mack saw people he didn't know or didn't know well whispering to their friends and pointing at him. And of course, there was his eye. That served to verify at least a part of the story. But whatever the actual content of the circulating accounts, surprisingly to Mack, he apparently was not being seen as the screw up he had imagined. Rather, if his friends were to be believed, the descriptive word being used most often was heroic.

Mack's initial conversation with Tad was typical, if in greater detail. They found some time while waiting for the film in Fletcher's history class to begin.

"Tad, help me out a little here. Am I misreading things or is everyone being extra nice to me?"

"Right. Though I wouldn't quite say everyone. Most kids think Coffin and Wenger and that crew had it coming. They're mostly glad someone was willing to take them on, even if it was, as some say, on behalf of Johnny Raymond."

"And you?"

"I was afraid you'd ask me." But even as he said that, he smiled. "You know I'm all for Johnny. The gay thing doesn't bother me. I just have one complaint." Mack took a deep breath and nodded. "Why didn't you ask me to come with you?"

"You serious?"

"Uh, yeah. Might have saved us losing our starting quarterback for a couple of games."

"There is that. I still can't quite believe Ames."

"Well, he did what he did and I can't say I like that any better than you, but—since you asked—most everyone is blaming him and maybe Coffin, not you. There are a few exceptions, of course, but that would be true no matter what."

And so it went, all day Wednesday general support—all around. Of course, a lot of kids wanted to hear the story directly from Mack. He was a bit uncomfortable with this, downplaying any hero talk. He tried to stick to the bare facts in his description of what had happened, attempting to end with something like "I was mostly just trying to do the right thing. I wish that things had turned out differently, without a fight I mean."

Most folks were content with a short version of the story, though a few pressed him for details. He tried to stay away from naming Johnny Raymond's part in things, but everyone seemed to know already, so there was little use in denying it. He managed a brief conversation with Johnny during the one class they shared.

It was on the order of "Ya doin' okay?"

"Yeah, you?"

*****

Thursday was different. A few minutes into first period, Fletcher called Mack up to his desk and said quietly, "Mr. Ames wants to see you in his office now."

With two minutes of walking between classroom and office, Mack barely had the time to wonder *what he had done wrong this time* before knocking on the VP's door. The face that greeted him did not look encouraging.

"Come in, McKyer. Sit down." Mack took his low-down seat in front of Ames's desk. "I understand," continued the VP, "that you are wandering about the building sharing your distorted view of Saturday night's events."

"But, Mr. Ames, I'm only tellin——"

"That'll do, McKyer. I thought we agreed last time you were here that when I want you to say something, I will ask. You are here to listen." Ames waited, briefly. Mack wanted to defend himself, but he knew better, so he also waited. "In case I have not made myself clear. From this point on, you are not to talk about the events of last Saturday night unless it's to say you know you only received the punishment you deserve. Now is *that* clear?"

"Is that a request for an answer, sir?"

"Don't get smart with me, young man. I asked you a question that requires an answer."

"Then you're saying, Mr. Ames, that if I say anything about Saturday night, I'm to lie about it."

"You are trying to twist my words, Mister McKyer," said Ames.

While simultaneously, Mack added, "If I say I'm getting punishment I deserve, then that's a lie. All I've said about Saturday is the truth."

"That'll be more than enough, McKyer. Obviously, you have not yet learned your lesson. I'll be adding another game to those you'll be missing next fall."

"But—"

"And if I hear one more word or one more report that you are continuing with these half-truths and innuendos—if that's a word you're familiar with—then you'll be out for the season, Mr. McKyer, the whole football season. You may leave."

Half in a daze, Mack wandered past the secretary's desk and opened the door to the hall. "Mack," the secretary called after him. "Wait a second. You'll need this hall pass to get back into class." She handed it to him and looked at him closely. "Are you all right?"

Mack shrugged. "Not really."

They stared at one another a moment longer. She looked like she wanted to say something further but then glanced toward the vice principal's door. Walking back to her desk to sit down, she looked again in Mack's direction. "I hope," she had started to add, "that your day gets better." But Mack had turned the corner and disappeared.

*****

That next to the last day of the school year had become more than awkward. He took his time walking back to class. What was he supposed to do? What was he supposed to say? Nothing seemed the only possible response. But how was that going to work? *Shit, what the hell? Goddamn it. That sanctimonious son of a bitch*, he thought. Mack rarely used those words out loud, except when he was really angry. In that quiet hall, he didn't use them here either. But if there was a place and time for them, now seemed to be one. *There were no kind or neutral words for Ames. I've been shat upon, screwed over, left up shit creek without a paddle. And it wasn't my goddamn fault.*

Keep on walkin', Mack. Walk right out that side door and don't look back.

But he had tried that. And where had it gotten him the last time? No, if he was going to keep walkin', he had to really mean it—not a day off in a cheap movie theater and another I'm-sorry-I-won't-do-it-again conference in the principal's office and not an I-don't-care-about-you-Mom-and-Dad disappearance act. If he was going to quit school or transfer or move back to Iowa on his own, then he had to be man enough to say that to everyone who mattered and then do it.

Ah, but what about those people who did care here in good old Columbia City? What about his friends, his parents, his teammates? Wouldn't this all be something for Darrel Coffin to brag about? *Ran that athlete hero right out of town, I did.* And what was the deal with Ames, anyway? He's a smart-enough guy. Got at least his master's degree, right? *But it obviously didn't teach him that listening was part of his job, listening and any kind of discernment about truth telling or apparently, any interest in justice or hearing anything that didn't fit with his biased view of things, or...or...or...*

Mack opened Fletcher's classroom door and entered a semi-darkened space while the latter half of a documentary on the Civil Rights movement of the 1960s flickered into life on the screen. He handed his excuse slip to the teacher and sat down at the back of the classroom. He had watched the film before for a project in one of his other classes. He supposed it was worth seeing again, but for most of that hour, his mind was elsewhere.

Mack mentally backed off his initial reaction. Leaving Lincoln was really not a good option for many reasons. He would be a senior next year, likely preparing for and making a choice about college. What kind of scholarship offers was he likely to get if he either quit or was suspended from school?

There were good chances that both the football and basketball teams, on which he was a key returning member, would be competing for championships. People were counting on him and he did not want to disappoint them. But more than that, he genuinely liked most of his fellow students. He liked his coaches and even a few of the regular teachers. He anticipated, even expected, to enjoy his last year in high school. Maybe that was a naive expectation, but he had thought it was a reasonable possibility. Now he wasn't nearly as confident. And if he couldn't walk or run away, he couldn't let things go either.

There must be some reasonable option going forward, some middle ground between quitting and surviving as is. But what? How could he convince Ames that he had had no choice to do other than what he had done? How could he even get the man to listen to him for more than three seconds? Then there was the niggling thought: What if he was more at fault here than he had been willing to admit to? Was he the arrogant, self-righteous shit Ames seemed to think he was? There was a spanner in the works, a fly in the ointment, water in the gas tank, a groundhog loose in the tomato patch, a rat in the woodpile. It was—as Ms. Parsons, Mack's English teacher, was known to say—a concept seeking a metaphor.

Mack tuned back into the Civil Rights film in time to see the infamous Edmund Pettis Bridge scene of the young Congressman-to-Be John Lewis being beaten soundly by law enforcement officials who then hauled him off to jail. *Now there was a cause worth a few bruises and a broken bone or two. I wonder if Lewis thought that at the time he was getting his head pounded on. More significant than my cause for sure,* thought Mack. *I wonder if what's going on here is important enough. Is there a principle here worth jeopardizing my athletic career? Is this a matter of my integrity or am I just being bullheaded? Do I fight this or accept the fact that vice principals hold all the high cards in the deck?*

The bell rang with no decision made or in sight. Perhaps if there had been another week or two left in the school year, Mack wouldn't have been able to let things be, but the only choice he was ready to make was to last the rest of the day and Friday morning without running further afoul of VP Ames. So he basically opted for a vow of silence. His friends could tell something was wrong. Others who didn't know him well might have gotten the impression that he thought himself too cool or above them to condescend to a conversation. To a very few, he said, "I can't talk about it right now. It's nothing personal. I'll tell you when I can."

*****

Mack's nonreactive stance was unsatisfying but did help him postpone decisions he was not ready to make. On Friday, the last day of his junior year, he managed to survive and he said some goodbyes, especially to the seniors he knew. At least for those reasons, the day wasn't a total waste. Nate Garvery was one of those goodbyes. So was "Skye" King. And so was Johnny Raymond. For those moments, though hardly forgotten, his troubles took a back seat.

"Hey, Nate. You made it! Congrats on the scholarship to the U and getting out of here."

"Hey yourself, man, good luck getting back to state next year. But you better prep well for the alumni game. That won't be a walk in the park. I'll guarantee it," he said with a smile.

"It won't be the same when we're on different sides. I'll miss ya, man." And surprise, he really meant it. There had been times earlier in the year when he was sure that day would never come.

"Don't forget us down in the hood. We'll be getting after it a few times a week at the center or one of the schoolyards. Just text me when that small ball stuff you're messin' with gets too boring. As for that new VP, if you can handle me, you can handle him." They exchanged a last high five as fellow high school students.

George "Skye" King found Mack trying to hide out in the library.

"Been lookin' for you," he said. "Saw you head this way." Skye was a big man of few words, so Mack suspected whatever he had to say would be well thought through. Still, he was both surprised and touched by King's words. "We come a long ways in the past couple of months, you and I," said Skye, "and I didn't want to leave Lincoln without saying thank you."

"That's unnecessa—"

"Stop. It is necessary. I want you to know for sure that it meant a lot to me—not just the stuff with the whole team and the mess with Nate. I was just as rough on you as he was, in a way, yet when I asked for help, you put that aside. You were there for me. That's it, man. That's all. Oh yeah, and I been hearin' stuff. Don't let the man get you down."

Mack was speechless for a moment. Then he stood up, still feeling like a midget next to Skye's 6'8" frame. He reached as far as he could in the air and gave Skye a resounding high-five slap before saying, "If this wasn't the school library, I'd give you hug or a chest bump." Skye looked him up and down, glanced briefly around to see if the librarian was watching. She was. But before anything else could be said, they both positioned themselves and jumped. Well, Mack jumped. Skye went tiptoed. And that was, the librarian reported later, the first chest bump she had ever seen in the library. "Boys," she said, "boys." But she smiled as she said it. "No use hiding in here anymore," said Mack as the next bell rang.

As for Johnny, saying goodbye was, of course, premature. The baseball season would continue for another month, and by mutual agreement, they would have time. "But," said Johnny, "there's a couple of things that won't wait. First, I really wanted to tell you face-to-face and haven't had the chance till now. Thanks for backing me up. I don't know where things would've ended that night if you hadn't showed up, but it sure wasn't looking good." Mack nodded and shrugged as in "What else could I do?" "Second, I can't substantiate this, but I heard via a friend who has another friend who goes to Ames's former school. Word there was he had a thing about athletes, especially football players. I don't know if that's too late for you to make a difference, but maybe knowing there's something goin' on that ain't about you will help on down the road."

Those last words of Johnny's were on his mind that Friday noon as Mack made his way out of Lincoln High for the last time of his junior year. It was Lincoln tradition that on the afternoon of the last day, school faculty, including the principal and other administrators, would line the main doorway of the school to wish all returning students a good summer. Of course, that could be avoided if the student wanted to leave quietly by one of the side doors, but it was a good tradition and most students kept it, according to Mack's friends. So he felt a bit of pressure to comply. And surely, he could avoid Ames if it came to that. And there he was, sighing and waiting his turn behind about fifty of the other returnees.

The wait was short. The tradition was well enough organized. All four doorways were in use with different faculty members to choose from. Coaches Smitson and Phillips were both on door number three, so Mack headed that way. Surely they were aware of what had been going on in Mack's life. Was it his imagination that both men looked at him with deep concern in their eyes as they wished him well for the summer? They exchanged a few other words, but longer conversation was not possible. Smitson asked Mack to give him a call and passed him a card with contact info on it. Mack said he would, but that was it.

Meanwhile, Principal Grandy and VP Ames were beyond the doors on the broad walkway outside patio basically trying to shake hands with everyone. Again, there obviously was little or no time for conversation. That, Mack assumed, was part of the plan. However, it would also be difficult to pass by unnoticed. Mack considered making the effort but decided that was a gutless choice and shook hands with the principal, who seemed to hold on to his handshake an extra moment with a look of some concern on his face. (Again, was this his imagination?)

Mack turned to VP Ames and said, "I hope you've had the time to think things through more clearly. Have a great summer!" *I hope I took the words he was about to say to me right out of his mouth*, he thought. Indeed, Mack had the satisfaction of watching a speechless Ames trying to come up with something to say while having to concentrate on shaking the next hand in front of him. Mack quickly turned away and left the vicinity, caught a glimpse of Kerry's red hair about twenty feet away in the crowd, and slipped through in his direction.

As they headed on home, Kerry asked what he had said to Ames. Mack told him and added, "I couldn't resist, and maybe I've blown it again. We'll see. How was your last day?"

CHAPTER 20

Attitude Adjustments

It was the Saturday of Memorial Day weekend. School was out. No game was scheduled because of the holiday. Mack decided to go for a long walk. He slipped out of the house without telling anyone and headed for Woodland Park. It was a bright, sunny, almost-summer morning. The air had a bit of chill to it, but that made for good, vigorous walking weather without hardly breaking a sweat. It had been an intensely difficult week and nothing much was yet resolved, but for the time being, what Mack felt was mostly relief. It was good to be out in the fresh air again with no particular agenda—at least none that needed his immediate attention. No homework, no dances, no games, and no vice principals on his case. Mack brought a notebook and a pen with him—no electronics. He thought maybe he would find something worth writing about, perhaps a witty poem or a profound comment on the human condition. Or not.

As Mack entered the park, the only poetic thought that occurred to him had something to do with the straight, tall evergreen trees that bordered most of the pathways where he walked. He had heard somewhere that many of these trees were four to five hundred years old. He wondered what their world was like back when they were first seeded or planted. He even imagined them walking about like those treelike creatures in the Tolkien books, what secrets they might have to tell. Eventually, he found a spot to sit surrounded by cedar trees with trunks large enough that it would take at least a basketball team to stretch their arms around one.

With such beings—Mack found it impossible to think of the trees as less than beings—he felt the limits of his age. He was not yet seventeen. Some of those trees were twenty-five times older than he. And when he grew older and died, most of them would still be here, still guardians of the park if the park was still a park. In a sense, such thoughts left him feeling very small indeed, like we sometimes feel gazing up at the stars on a clear and cloudless night away from the city or sifting through the rocks turned into a gazillion acres of sand by the eons-old pounding of the ocean tides.

Mack did not feel small in the sense of invaluable or discounted by size or age. Rather, he felt his value, his purpose in human terms, and yet still akin to those trees. He didn't have the history or the roots of the great trees, but he did have history and roots. He came from something, from human seed if you will, and he was becoming something. He just didn't know what yet. And the trees and their ageless fulfilling of their purpose gave Mack an inkling of hope that he would find his own—someday.

Some perspective began to emerge. He couldn't solve the world's problems, even the problems of his small world. It was certainly unlikely he would be able to change VP Ames. But he could resolve to be the best Mack he could be. That would have to be enough for now. Not that he yet knew what that would look like exactly.

Still under that huge cedar tree, Mack dug through his notebook for a piece of paper he had slipped in there when he headed out on his walk. It was a copy of the speech Coach Smitson had given out to the team after the end of the football season last November.

"In all sports," he read, "particularly at the higher competitive levels, athletes are challenged to find a way to focus their talent and energy toward the goal or purpose of the game they are playing. There are three vital dimensions that make for success in athletics. They are the physical gifts of the individual, the time devoted to practice, and the developed ability to focus. There are many physically gifted athletes who practice faithfully but never learn to focus. They may enjoy their participation in sports. They will develop their skill set beyond that of those who expect to do so without practice. They may learn to play well with others. In fact, it could easily be argued that the overall purpose of sports is the value of play for play's sake, the value of learning to work together with a team toward a common goal, and of course, the value of learning to both win and lose with grace. But there are many for whom this is not enough. That is where the power to focus comes into play."

So, Mack asked himself, *am I one of those "for whom this is not enough"?* It was the first time he could remember actually thinking about why athletics had been so important in his life. In the past, he hadn't gotten much further than "playing for the love of the game." He couldn't remember not wanting to compete, to measure his athletic skills with those of his childhood friends and increasingly, with peers he knew only through organized competition. From the day he bought his first pack of baseball cards, he had dreamed of becoming a professional ballplayer with his own face on one of those cards, complete with career statistics printed on the back. A common dream for a young American boy? Yes, and probably a foolish one if not relinquished—most of the time. But not always.

As Mack got a bit older and discovered the enjoyment of watching various sports on television or catching the occasional professional or college game in person, awareness gradually dawned. Very, very few people were good enough in their sport to reach and find success in professional sports. Even collegiate athletic participation was limited to a relatively small number of the population. And as if he didn't need to remind himself further, not everyone who wanted to and thought themselves good enough made their high school teams either. There was a weeding-out process that gradually separated those who played a sport mostly for fun and those who aspired to something more.

Factored into this interior exploration were some of the discussions he had with fellow athletes, particularly Nate Garvery, Lamont Stevens, and Kerry Fergeson. Of those three, Kerry and Lamont were both three sport athletes, like Mack had always thought of himself. Nate was almost totally focused on basketball. He also was, in Mack's assessment, the only one who might have a shot at a professional career. Were those two things connected? *I am so naive in some ways,* Mack reflected. *Why have I never even thought this through? If I want to reach the highest level of a sport, wouldn't it make pure sense to focus on that sport and let go of the others?*

In his dialogue with himself, Mack quickly responded internally to his last question, *There are a couple of reasons. First, I like playing all three major American sports. In fact, I like playing most any game that involves a ball of some sort. Second, in team sports, the players work with and come to count on their teammates. How, for example, would I be able to look Kerry and Lamont, Coach Smithson, and all the rest of the football team in the eyes next September and say I've decided I didn't want to be a football player any longer? I'm going to focus on what? Which? And here's a crazy addendum to this—if I'd have been asked a year ago which sport I would choose if I could only play one, the choice would have been baseball—the only one I'm apparently not good enough to play at the high school level.*

And three, maybe it is time to decide that playing a sport is a great form of exercise, a way to enjoy a competitive experience, something to talk about with other guys. And that's enough. There are more important things in life than scoring a winning touchdown, hitting a grand slam, or making a triple double. Lots of people play their last really competitive games in Little League or in high school. Sports are not my only career choice.

And that's about where the conversation broke down or at least ceased for the moment. *Fortunately,* Mack concluded, *I don't have to decide anything right now. Yeah, right, I have at least six weeks.*

He texted Coach Smitson, "Hi, coach. I'm very interested in getting together for a conversation. Do you have any free time next week? I have baseball games Tuesday and Saturday and work fifteen to twenty hours other afternoons and evenings but can make time most any morning."

Coach replied to Mack, "Hi, Mack. Good to hear from you. How about next Wednesday? School's out, but I'll be in my gym office taking care of a few leftover things. You can stop by there about 10:00 a.m. unless you have another place in mind."

*****

He texted Johnny Raymond, "Hey, Johnny. Hope you are as glad as I am that the turmoil is over for now. Would you like to get back to our pitching practice? Doing anything for the holiday weekend? How about 2:00 p.m. Sunday? 11:00 a.m. Monday? Or touch base at Tuesday's game? You choose."

Johnny replied to Mack, "Not sure that the pitching thing is going to work out, but I figure I owe you one. Weather permitting, I'll see you Sunday at two at the alma mater."

*****

The usual pattern for the extra practice session with Johnny held. When Mack arrived at the stroke of two, Johnny had obviously been there for a while. He was jogging around the empty field and waved when he saw Mack arrive with his bag of baseball gear. Johnny sprinted over in his direction near the first base dugout.

"Hey," he said after catching his breath, "seems like it's been a lot longer than a week since our last get together."

"Yeah," Mack replied, "I hope you're okay."

"Well, I haven't managed to get my head stuck in any toilets recently."

"Ha! I'm done with mentioning that if you are. I was more hoping you were okay with continuing these extra practice sessions. You weren't exactly enthusiastic at the end of our last one."

"True. And I have thought about it—quite a lot, actually. I know you've been right all along about our team pitching. It _is_ our biggest weakness. And until you suggested this"—Johnny gestured around the field for a moment—"I guess I didn't really care. I mean I know I can pitch, but I just didn't/don't want to be the center of attention. You see what it's like—not always—but some of the time when I'm at bat, and people start the Johnny Rainbow—shit. Can you imagine it if I were on the mound for the whole or even part of a game? I don't need that. I play baseball because it's fun and I'm good at it. When it stops being fun, I'll stop playing. I don't need the aggravation—even if it means a better won-loss record."

"I think I'm hearing a yes, but."

Johnny grinned. "Hey, you're pretty good at this listening-behind-the-words stuff. You're right, again. Especially after this last week, more than ever, I want a crack at those high school high and mighty jocks—present company accepted—and to get that we've got to win a lot more games." Mack nodded.

"Then," Johnny went, "there's you and your arm. You're faster than I am." Mack shook his head. "Really, you are. But you need to work on getting one of your breaking pitches over the plate consistently and you do need to develop a better changeup—especially for a few of those high school hitters who tend to like fastballs."

"Okay. I like how you're sounding right now and there are two things I need to say back. The first is this, do you know what baseball people call players who react to loudmouthed fans?"

Johnny thought for maybe six seconds. "Rabbit ears?"

"Right. So—no harsh criticism intended—I don't know how I would be reacting if fans were calling Francis Rainbow every time I touched the ball. No, listen," he said as Johnny laughed—an actual long, drawn-out belly laugh.

Johnny added, "I do keep forgetting your first name really is Francis."

"Listen," Mack tried again, "if you do get to the place where you are willing to try pitching in a game, I want us to have a strategy that we can put into play that will support you and maybe help when you're not pitching. I have a couple of ideas, but we can get to those later. Meanwhile, I want to repeat what I did over a week ago now. You are already good enough to pitch—probably on the college level IF YOU WANT TO. I'm not just blowing smoke here. I mean it. But I also mean that I will not try to pressure you directly or indirectly. It will be your choice. Well, and my dad's, of course, since he has the final say for the dear old Yellow Jackets."

"All right," Johnny said, "that's enough BS for the time being. You brought a whole bag of balls. After warm-ups, let's each do a little throwing to an actual live batter this time."

*****

Tuesday couldn't get there soon enough for Mack. Given the time of year, school was now a past topic. For the time being, Lisa was forgotten. Elana was forgotten. For the moment, even VP Ames was forgotten. For the first time since the beginning of the season, Mack felt like he could concentrate on baseball. Except for that brief premature comeback against Charlie's Angels, it would be more than three weeks since he had last played. His hand was not yet 100 percent, but it was better. The workouts with Johnny had helped. His pitching control was improving and he could grip a bat and hit a ball without flinching.

It was more than simple physical well-being. Mack remembered a time, not so many years ago, when from April through August he "ate, slept, and dreamt" baseball—watched far too many pro games and highlights, collected tons of memorabilia, and played the game as often as he could, even if it was to throw balls at a wall or catch with his dad when a pickup game with friends was not available. As he and his dad got into the car for the drive to the field for Tuesday's game against the First Responders, he was excited about playing in an actual baseball game for the first time since last summer in Iowa. It would be fair to say that he had undergone an attitude adjustment— at least with respect to baseball.

CHAPTER 21

An Unexpected Debut

The Yellow Jackets were nearing the halfway point in the season and so far, they were—to use Mack's father's terms—mired in mediocrity. They had started out fine with a three-game winning streak but had currently lost four in a row. This would be their third game with the First Responders who had reeled off six wins after losing to the YJs in that first wild contest of the season. The FRs were in first place by themselves at 6–1, followed by Charlie's Angels at 5–2. No one else in the league had a winning record thus far. The YJs were tied with the Grand Salamis and the Callapa Bay Oysters at 3–4.

They had now played every team at least once, and by Mack's assessment, if (and it was a big if) the YJs could improve their pitching, they had a very good chance of moving up in the standings. He had yet to tell his dad about his and Johnny's workouts. He really didn't want his dad to bank on either of them at this point. Maybe another week or so and probably, it would make a lot of sense for both he and Johnny, if Johnny was willing, to pitch seriously at a couple of YJ practices. Better to bring the team on board to, hopefully, build up their confidence before surprising everyone in a game situation.

Thus, not that Coach/Dad knew he had a choice yet, it would be Softstuff against the First Responders again. Mack was afraid this would not be a good thing, but he didn't know what to do about it.

During the first three innings, the bats were quiet for both teams. Softstuff was doing a good job of keeping the ball down in the strike zone, and the First Responders obliged by hitting a lot of ground balls to the infield. Mack had handled four chances at short, though only one was hit very hard. Against the First Responder southpaw, the YJs were not much better. They had managed only two hits and no runs. Mack led off the third inning with a solid single and stole second but died there when the next two batters struck out and the third flied to left.

Things changed dramatically in the fourth. In the visitor's half of the inning, Alan Alford opened the scoring with a home run barely inside the foul pole in left. Sam Jackson followed with a double off the fence in right center. It looked like he might remain at second when the next batter, Stan Borison, popped up to first and Georgeena Daniels struck out. But Randal James slashed a ground ball single through the right side. Jackson scored, and on the throw to the plate, Randal took second. Up next, Mack worked the count full and drove the 3–2 pitch off the top of the wall in left center. He came within a foot of having his first home run of the season. James scored, making it 3–0 YJs, but Morgan grounded out weakly to the pitcher for the third out. There the score remained for another inning.

In the First Responder half of the fifth, Morgan struggled with his usually sound control and walked the first two batters. The third hitter made him pay with a shot that barely cleared Johnny's glove in deep center scoring the two men on base. He slid into third with a triple and then tied the score on a sacrifice fly to left. The First Responders did not appear to be done when the next two hitters continued the rally with a pair of singles. With runners on first and third and two outs, the Responder cleanup hitter was up. Softstuff had kept him hitless thus far, but the man definitely looked capable. He stepped into the batter's box, took a couple of practice swings, and eyed Morgan like he was ready to take his head off. And that's when, for a moment, things went quite crazy—as they sometimes do in baseball.

With the count 1–1, Softstuff tried to run his curveball just off the inside corner of the plate. Unfortunately, the ball broke through the heart of the plate and the cleanup hitter was ready for it. He hit the ball very hard, a low line drive headed up the middle toward center. The only thing in the way was the pitcher and the ball didn't take his head off, but it did hit him on the right side and bounced away toward the YJ dugout. Softy fell to the ground moaning. With two outs, the base runners had been off with the pitch. The one on third scored easily and the runner on first made it all the way around to third. With Larry Chen and Randal James scrambling to chase down the ball in short right field, the batter landed on second, standing up. Chen came racing in with the ball in time to hold the runners where they were. Time was quickly called, and everyone on the infield and the bench gathered around Softstuff who was still lying on the ground.

The first thing was, of course, to check on whether Softy was still in one piece, much less if he could remain in the game. One of the EMTs on the Responder's bench came over to check him out. He even had a stethoscope with him and insisted on giving the pitcher a bit of an exam. When Softy was finally able to take a couple of normal breaths and actually stand up, the EMT announced him fit enough. Coach McKyer was not so sure. The ophthalmologist, Dr. Larry Chen, was not so sure either. Softy confirmed his fitness by throwing a couple of practice pitches and told the team he was ready to give it a go. Three pitches later, a routine fly ball to Johnny in center ended the inning, stranding the two base runners and leaving the score at 4–3 First Responders.

While the middle of the YJ batting order was trying to create some difficulties for the FR pitcher, the greater drama was taking place on the YJ bench. Mack's dad was sitting next to Softstuff Morgan, who was not looking decidedly better. He was rubbing his side and listening to Karl McKyer.

"Listen, Softy, this is just a ball game and not exactly the World Series. It's not worth aggravating your body for another inning or two. We'll work things out. You need to get yourself to an ER or outpatient clinic. In fact, I think I will drive you to one."

"You ain't drivin' me nowhere. You got to stay here and manage—if I go, that is."

"Damn it, Softy. You are in no shape to get back out there or to drive yourself anywhere."

"But I know you were counting on me to go the distance today—especially since Jason is out of town."

At that point, two others entered the discussion with what became a key turning point in the YJ season, although no one knew it at the time.

Pepper Wexler asked, "Hey, are you going to need me today? If not, I'll be glad to take Softy for a ride to the ER."

"But—" Softstuff got out of his mouth before Johnny Raymond's interruption.

"Coach Karl, I don't know if you know this, but you have a really good relief pitcher sitting on the bench."

Everyone who heard looked around as if to say, "Where?"

"Actually, he's your current shortstop and waiting on deck to hit."

"Mack?" Coach Karl said with some incredulity.

"Yeah, Mack. We've been working out together, and I've been catching him off the mound at the high school field for the last few weeks. He's ready."

"You're sure?" Johnny nodded. Softy nodded to Pepper. Pepper nodded to anyone else who was looking. And when Mack returned to the bench after a disappointing fly out to right center, he received one of the major surprises of his young athletic life.

"Mack," his dad said, "Softy is going to the doctors and you're going in to pitch. Josh, grab a catcher's glove and see if you can get Mack a few extra warm-up tosses in."

Mack caught Johnny's eye for a moment, saw the shake of his head, and headed off to the bullpen warm-up area slightly down the third baseline. For better or worse, his pitching career was about to begin.

That first inning on the mound went better than anyone, including Mack, expected. His initial concern was a determination to throw strikes. Before his first pitch, Mack told Sam Jackson that he wanted to stick with his fastball as much as possible and that's what he did. He was helped by having to face only the last third of the First

Responder batting order and they each cooperated by waiting him out for two strikes. The first two then ground weakly to the infield. The third struck out, swinging on three straight fastballs. Mack left the hill feeling pretty good. He was, however, not thrilled by the team response, which was a lot of backslapping affirmation. He did not want them to think of him as a new incarnation of Matt Scherzer or some other star hurler of more recent fame. "Time to relax," said Jackson, "and take a few deep breaths." He reminded them that they were still behind and that the strongest First Responder hitters were coming up in the next inning.

Sam Jackson sat beside Mack during the YJ's half of the seventh. He put an arm over Mack's shoulder and said, "Congrats. I didn't know you were a pitcher." Mack laughed.

"I didn't know I was one either."

"Okay. Well, you sure looked like one a moment ago. You got anything beside that fastball you're gonna want to try?"

"I've been working on a slider, a slow curve, and a straight change, but control is still an issue."

"Let's stick with the fastball then until they start catching up to it. That may take another inning or two. But just in case, let's at least pretend that we've got signals we're paying attention to. Without a runner on second, we'll use the tried and true one finger down for the fastball, two for the curve, and three for a changeup. Shake me off every now and then, even if you're throwing the fastball. That will make them think a little bit anyway. With a runner on second, a closed fist at any time will erase everything but the fastball. If I think we need to try something different, I'll call time and we'll talk. Sound all right to you?"

"Yeah, but I got a couple of questions. What about the slider? And do you want to have a signal for a pickoff move?"

"When I signal for a curve, throw the slider if you want. All I really need to know is if it's going to be a breaking pitch. I can adjust to the speed on my own. For a pickoff signal, let's leave that to the next time we have practice. We can work something out then. For now, just remember to hold any runners close. Go ahead and make a throw to first if the runner is stretching a lead. Don't fake it. Unless your foot is off the rubber, that's a balk. And you know, of course, that you can fake a throw to second without making a balk. You'll be fine. You know all this stuff. You just haven't had to think about it much before. Oh, and two other things. First, as much as possible, when you're ready to throw, keep your eyes on my glove. That's your target. I may move around a bit after the batter is in the box, but I'll stay put when you go into your windup. And second, don't forget we're supposed to be having fun out here."

"Right. Thanks."

"Mack," Jackson said, "you know I'm a high school baseball coach, right?" Mack nodded. "Based on what I'm seeing, you could be pitching for any high school team in the city—now. Don't forget that."

As Sam was talking, Mack glanced over at Johnny. *That's almost exactly what I told him more than once*, he thought.

The score was still 4–3 when Mack took the hill in the last of the seventh. As planned, he almost exclusively used his fastball. The First Responder leadoff man fouled off a couple of pitches but struck out when he lunged for a ball out of the strike zone. The next batter hit the first pitch up the middle, but Mack deflected the ball toward Larry Chen, now playing short. Larry bare-handed the ball and threw the runner out by a couple of steps. On a 2–2 pitch, the number three hitter lifted a very high fly ball to straightaway center—no problem for Johnny.

Mack led off the YJ eighth inning with a sharp single to left center. He thought about trying to stretch it for a double but wisely decided against it. The throw from left came in straight and sure to the Responder second baseman. On a 1–1 count, Josh Kelsey, batting in Morgan's position, laid a bunt down the first baseline. He was out easily, but Mack was safe at second. That brought up Johnny Raymond who slapped a high outside fastball straight down the line in right. Mack scored standing up, and Johnny coasted into second. Chen popped up to short, and Alford flied out to short left, but Sam Jackson drove Johnny home with a drive into the gap in right center. Borison fouled out to the catcher, but the YJs now led 5–4.

In the Responder half of the eighth, Mack gave up his first hit. The cleanup hitter for the FRs caught up to one of Mack's fastballs and sent the ball to the base of the wall in deep center. Johnny's speed and throw kept the runner at second. But no one was out, and for the first time, Mack lost his focus and walked the next batter on four pitches. To compound matters, Mack forgot to check the runners, and on his first pitch to the next hitter, both advanced a base on a double steal. Things did not look good. Runners were now on second and third with only one out.

At that point, Sam came out to the mound for a brief chat. Nothing of much meaning was said. "This is mostly a time," Jackson said to Mack, "for you to take a few deep breaths." That he did or almost. After a ball-one count, Mack was determined to throw a strike and let up a bit on his fastball. The Responder hitter didn't miss it. He hit the ball on a line directly toward Josh Kelsey, now playing third. Kelsey really had no time to think. Pure reflexes came into play. The ball stuck in his glove. Kelsey hurriedly stepped on third before the runner could retreat. And Mack learned why the double play is a pitcher's best friend.

The ninth inning was almost anticlimactic. For the YJs, Georgeena Daniels singled but died at first when Randy and Mack flied out and Kelsey ground out to second. The Responders needed one run for a tie, two for the win. Facing the bottom of the order again, with the first batter, Mack tried his slow curve on a 2–2 count. It was well outside the strike zone, but the batter swung anyway for another strikeout, the first of three Mack needed to end the game. He tried too hard and walked the next guy up. One out and a runner on first.

In the pitcher's spot, the Responders sent up a pinch hitter who looked like a guy who could hit the ball a long way if he got hold of one. Sam came out for another chat. His advice was to waste a fastball outside and then go to the slow curve. Mack followed his catcher's suggestions. The first pitch was a bit outside, and the batter let it go for ball one. Mack tried to appear nonchalant about it, but inside, he was thrilled when the curve caught the inside corner for a called strike. The second curve broke off the plate for ball two. A third curve caught the outside corner to even the count at 2–2. Sam then called for the fastball again. The batter, likely looking for the curve, swung hard but too late. The ball was already in Jackson's glove.

The Responder leadoff hitter had been a pain to the Yellow Jackets all game. He was three for four with two runs scored. When Mack forgot to check, the runner on first immediately stole second. Mack was disgusted at himself but tried not to let it show. Now a single could tie the score. Briefly, Mack felt another attack of nerves, took a deep breath, and leaned in for the sign. Stan flashed a bunch of different signs that Mack pretended to consider followed by a closed fist. *Ah, he wants the fastball.* Mack nodded, looked the runner back toward second, toed the rubber, took his stretch, and fired his fastball right over the middle of the plate. Then to the shock of everyone on the YJs, the batter bunted the ball with two outs. He pushed the bunt down the first-base side, where both infielders were playing back. The only one who had a play on the ball was Mack. He raced to his left and went into a slide with the hope of cutting the ball off and flipping it to Randal at first. And he booted the ball, knocking it toward the first-base dugout, jumped back to his feet, and chased it down.

The runner from second hadn't stopped at third but had headed home and was halfway there before Mack could pick up the ball. Mack's back was turned and he didn't see the runner, but he did hear Sam Jackson's desperate call. "Home, Mack, home." Mack had no time to think about it. He spun and fired a strike to Sam, who put the tag on the runner just before he reached the plate. Everyone's eyes quickly looked toward the umpire whose fist was raised in the air signaling an out. Sometimes it's better to be lucky than good.

Mack had won his first game as a pitcher, and the YJs had evened up their record at 4–4. They also now knew that they had another option for their pitching rotation. And they had yet another option that only two of them knew about.

CHAPTER 22

You Win Some And

The following Wednesday morning, Mack ate a leisurely breakfast and was lounging around in a bathrobe, watching SportsCenter and checking out social media on his phone. It was 9:45 a.m. when he suddenly remembered that he was supposed to be meeting football Coach Ed Smitson at the high school in about fifteen minutes. He raced back upstairs and threw on some sweats.

Both family cars were gone. Mack thought about grabbing his old bike, but a brief check of the tires suggested that was not a good idea. *Hmm, it's something like a half mile*, he thought. Mack glanced at a clock. *It's five minutes before ten. I should be able to make it in about four minutes.* So without further thought, he took off running. Short on breath, he arrived at the outside door to the gym about a minute after 10:00 a.m. *Guess I'm going to have to do some more running. I'm not in football or basketball shape anymore. But I did manage to put off thinking about what I'm going to say to coach.*

Mack tried the backdoor handle to the gym. It was unlocked. He entered that now-familiar space with mixed emotions. *Let's see. Only a little over two months since that day they posted the baseball team members for this year and I ran away from it all—briefly. Two months and it feels like two years. I've managed to avoid being here since then.* He barely had time to wonder—again—*what Smitson would have to say and what difference it would make*, and then he was there at the coach's office. The door was open.

Coach Smitson looked up from some reading in front of him. "Hi, Mack. Come on in and have a seat." Smitson set his reading aside. For a moment, they both looked each other over carefully as though they could imagine what the other was thinking or possibly anticipate where this crucial conversation might lead. The coach continued. "It's been a while since we've had more than hi to say to each other. So before we get to the stuff I need to talk about and probably you do, too, how are you, really? And try to make your response more than fine," he added with a smile.

"I'll try. I'm all right. Making it to the end of the school year was a relief, but that's almost getting to the stuff you were referring to. Otherwise, I've got a decent job for the summer. You probably know I'm playing baseball in the commercial league with my dad's team. That's been fun."

"Actually, I didn't know that. I remember being a bit surprised that you weren't on the high school team. But I guess you decided two full-time major sports were enough."

"I tried out. I didn't make the team."

"Really?" Smitson actually looked confused.

"I thought you knew."

"I probably should have. I missed the tryouts and didn't even see the team lists until they handed me the B-team roster after they were finalized. Funny that Hanson and Ramsey didn't mention it."

"Yeah." There was a pause, and the coach looked like something else had occurred to him and he was trying to decide whether to say anything more. Instead, he took a deep breath and asked a question, "Ready for that other stuff?"

Mack nodded. "Where do you want me to start?"

"How about you just tell me what happened?"

"I'm assuming you've already heard at least one version of that story—probably straight from the VP."

Smitson nodded. "But I would like to hear it in your words."

So Mack told him, beginning with observing Johnny heading toward the boy's room followed by the other guys, then ending with the meeting in Ames's office the following Monday and the follow-up meeting Thursday before school let out for the summer.

Then he added, "I've now had some time to think about it all from a bit of distance. And I can add that to the story if you want to hear it." Smitson nodded again. "Ames didn't want to hear it." Here, some of Mack's well-buried anger emerged in his tone of voice. "Ames didn't want to hear anything from me, actually. Every time I tried to explain my take on what had happened, he basically shut me down. So finally, I gave up. It was that or give up the whole football season. Once he discovered that taking away football games was how he could hurt me, that is what he used. And that I'm sorry about, coach. In trying to defend myself, I've hurt you and the team as well."

"Easy, Mack. Knowing you, I suspected that there was a fuller story I needed to hear. And I was right. But what about that added thinking you've been doing?"

"Okay, so basically three things—all optional responses and versions of what I could have done differently. Although, I need to start by saying that my immediate takeaway was that if I had the same situation before me, I would probably do exactly what I did. But the conferences with Ames—if that's what you can call them—did push me to think hard about choices in difficult situations.

"So first option, I could have done what Ames seemed to be pushing as the obvious choice. I could have immediately asked a teacher or chaperone to check things out instead of doing that on my own. Although I'm quite certain that would have taken more time than Johnny had. Plus I wasn't sure there was actually the kind of bullying situation unfolding that I suspected. What if all those guys simply needed to use the restroom to pee or freshen up or whatever? Then I'd have been a fool to report them, wouldn't I?

"Second, once I got to the boy's room door and saw that kid attempting to keep everyone out, I could have run back to the dance and found that chaperone or even Ames himself, but then once again, the time factor comes into play. If there was something dire going on, did I really have time to fetch someone to get the help needed? Turned out it was a dire situation—at least I saw it that way. A kid who had done absolutely nothing having a couple of bullies dunking his head in a toilet with several other guys standing around watching. If that's okay, then I really am a fool. Still, I could have taken that sergeant-at-arms kid's word that it wasn't my business and gone back to the dance or said something to a chaperone. That was a choice.

"Finally, I could have, as I'm sure my kindergarten teacher would have suggested, used my words instead of getting into the fight. In a way, I did try that. I told Coffin and Wenger to stop what they were doing before I attempted to interfere. Of course, that all happened pretty fast, so they might get away with saying that they would have stopped if I hadn't forced the issue. Yes, I could have, by my presence, just been a witness to their bad behavior and reported them later. No telling what all five of them would have said, though it's likely it would have been five versus two versions of the truth. So, coach, if that was your friend having his head stuffed in a toilet, would you have just watched?"

"No, Mack. No, I wouldn't have. I can still wish that you had taken option one or two since I'd probably still have my quarterback for the first three games of the season. But hearing your story and knowing the kind of kid you are, I don't see how you could have done things differently. The question is this: Can I convince Mr. Ames of that?"

"But you will try."

"I will, though there are no guarantees. He will, of course, see that I have a vested interest in believing you. And it will be tough for a man like him to go back on a decision he clearly thinks was correct and fair. He will likely think that would make him look weak and not the strong disciplinarian his position calls for and something else for you to think about. We will need to come up with an alternative plan in case he decides that your nonparticipation includes practices as well as the first three games of the season."

"Great. You're right. I hadn't thought about that at all."

Though nothing had essentially changed, Mack felt a whole lot better after that hour with Smitson. An adult, not his parent, and a person he respected believed him and not only that, would actually "go to bat for him"—*great baseball metaphor, that.* On whether the support of his old coach would make any difference in the vice principal's disciplinary decisions, Mack remained skeptical. When push came to shove, didn't all teachers and staff pretty much stick together? Wasn't that basically school politics and hadn't he already learned that the hard way?

Still, for now, he had done all he could. It was plain silly to think absolutely anything would happen while school was out for the summer. The decision to forget about Ames and Coffin and Wenger and Johnny and everything connected with them now felt like a no-brainer. He needed to get on with his life and leave the mess of the last couple of months behind. For a brief moment, he even forgot about baseball. But five minutes later, he remembered the old sports cliché: There is always another game. In fact, there was one in three days. *I wonder if I'll get another chance to pitch.*

*****

Coach/Dad silenced Mack's wondering on Friday. "Would you feel okay about starting our next game? I want to give Softstuff at least a week off. He's okay—nothing broken—but he's got a couple of bruised ribs and it still hurts him to take a deep breath. He said he'd throw if we needed him, but what do ya think?"

"Sure. Might as well find out if Tuesday was a fluke."

"You know, I always thought you had the arm, but you never seemed that interested in pitching. I was surprised when you didn't resist giving it a go Tuesday. What changed your mind?"

Well, crap! What a quandary! I can't very well tell him without going back on my promise to Johnny, he thought.

"What's the matter—cat got your tongue?"

"Now that is a ridiculous expression. Where do you come up with them anyway? What's a cat got to do with anything?"

"I don't really know. Maybe it's got something to do with the rough edges on cat's tongues. You know how they wash themselves and stuff."

"The way you said it, it didn't sound like you were talking about a cat's tongue but what cats could possibly do to a human tongue."

"I guess if one got a hold of mine, I probably wouldn't be able to talk, so what were we talking about anyway?"

"Uh, nothing much. Gotta run, Dad. See you at the game if not before."

*****

Johnny and Mack had planned to arrive about a half hour early to get in some extra work on their pitching before the YJ game with the Swedish Meatballs. For the first Saturday in June, in Columbia City, USA, it was unseasonably warm—a downright hot 87 degrees. The two of them were warming up their arms in the left-field bullpen area. Mack was pitching. Johnny was playing the catcher's part. Mack wasn't anywhere near throwing his hardest, but already, the sweat was pouring off his body. He called a halt.

"Let's take a break, grab some water, and sit in the shade for a while. I'll start throwing again when Sam gets here." They got a couple of water bottles from the dugout and then walked out to the shadow of the old oak tree just outside the left-field foul pole.

"Hey, man," said Johnny, "your slider and changeup are comin' along. You gonna use 'em much today?"

"Probably. I'll stick with the fastball most of the time, but I do want to try throwing the others just to keep the hitters off balance I still wish you'd, oops, sorry. I said I'd leave that alone."

"It's all right. I'm over being Mr. Sensitive about it. But reminder: I'm not ready yet so don't go sayin' anything about my pitching to your dad."

"I won't, but you won't stop me imagining you taking on the high school team and taking care of business for nine innings. You could do that right now, ya know. I know you could."

"Maybe. We'll see. And I still want to talk with you about the other stuff. You know."

"Anytime. How about after tomorrow's workout? Okay?"

Johnny nodded. "There's Sam. You better get back to throwing. Good luck. And Sunday. Same time. Same place."

*****

Twenty minutes later, the announcement came over the loud speaker system, "Batteries for today's game. For the visiting Columbia City Sporting Goods Yellow Jackets, Francis McKyer and Samuel Jackson. For the home team Swedish Meatballs, Mark Bonner and John Nelson. Let's play ball!" The tinny sounding sound system wasn't exactly major league, but it kind of felt good to Mack to hear his name as the starting pitcher for the first time, even if it was as Francis.

The game started as Mack had envisioned it—for the first two hitters in the Meatballs order that is. Both popped up to the infield. However, the third hitter in the order laced one of Mack's fastballs off the left-field fence and the fourth hitter knocked the ball over that same fence, 2–0 Meatballs. That was a rude awakening. *There would be no no-hitter today. Maybe I was just lucky against the Responders.* Telling himself to *bear down* seemed to work okay for a while. The score remained 2–0 until the top of the fifth when the Yellow Jacket offence finally got untracked. With two outs, Pepper Wexler, playing second, reached on an error. Mack doubled into the right center gap scoring Pepper. Johnny walked. Both of them advanced a base on a wild pitch, and Larry Chen singled them both home. Alford closed the scoring with a home run to left, and the YJs led 5–2. That score held until the bottom of the eighth.

Maybe if he was the sort of person to do so, Mack could have blamed that last inning on the heat or perhaps on the home-plate umpire who seemed to be calling Mack's lower pitches in the strike zone all balls or on bad defense. Pitching a whole game was, as he now knew firsthand, heavy duty. He did feel hot and tired and later, he would add, unfocused. In any case, things generally fell apart. Mack's control deserted him. The usually steady Larry Chen committed two errors at short. Stan Borison lost a fly ball in the sun in deep right field. All told, three errors, three walks, and the timely hitting of the Meatballs led to four runs. The YJ offense floundered again. The SMs walked off with a 6–5 victory. And Francis McKyer lost his first game as a starting pitcher.

To say he was disappointed would definitely be an understatement. *What happened out there? Was I overconfident? Okay, maybe a little. Did I really expect to breeze through my first game as a starting pitcher unscathed? Possibly. Man, I couldn't even throw anything but my medium-speed fastball in the strike zone and I couldn't even do that in the last inning. I was right back when the season started, and I told Dad I wasn't a pitcher. What on earth made me think I could walk up on a little hill sixty feet, six inches away from a seventeen-inch-square rubber plate and have absolutely no trouble throwing a small five ounce, nine inch in circumference red-stitched cowhide sphere over that plate between the knees and slightly above the waistline of a typical ballplayer?*

Of course, Mack's teammates were not nearly as hard on him as he was on himself. Larry Chen and Stan Borison both claimed responsibility for the loss. Several others were unhappy about their inability to produce hits in opportune moments—i.e., with runners in scoring position. What was the old team sports saying? You win as a team. You lose as a team. But like the quarterback in football and even a basketball point guard, the pitcher in baseball is the dominant figure. S/he handles the ball on every play. S/he sets the whole thing in motion. If s/he doesn't do his/her job well, then the team is likely to lose. Of course, it's a given that the team might find other ways to lose besides bad pitching. However, in this case, despite the input of teammates, Mack was prepared to shoulder the burden of the day's loss.

It was Peter Softstuff Morgan who provided Mack with the most helpful observations. Before changing his spikes into street shoes, Mack collapsed for a few minutes on the dugout bench. He was exhausted and though at pains to hide it, he felt like crying. Morgan plunked down beside him and threw an arm over his shoulder.

"Hey, man," he said, "I'm not saying this will make it any easier for you, but do you know how many games I've pitched and lost?" Mack, of course, shook his head. "To be entirely truthful, I'm not really sure, but I can guarantee it's been a lot—maybe as many as I've won, probably something in the neighborhood of a thousand. I admit it's usually more fun to win. I'm sure you've heard people say that baseball is a game where even the best hitters are only successful about one third of the time. We pitchers can surely be thankful for that fact. But it is also a major truth that not a single one of the best

Major League pitchers in all of history have finished a season with no losses. And most of the time, they—the best ones—lose more than half of the number they win. Check it out. Just sayin'. I'm guessing you'll be okay tomorrow. And you are—if you don't mind my saying so—already a more than okay hurler. Hang in there. I'm not that eager to get my old job back."

"Thanks, Peter."

CHAPTER 23

Pitching Options

Mack put in full-time work shifts Wednesday through Friday. He hung out with Red and watched a couple of ball games with him. He and Johnny met for their regularly scheduled pitching practice on Thursday after work. And during some spare time, he tried, rather unsuccessfully, to get into the summer reading list put out by the Lincoln High senior curriculum group. But mostly, his thinking focused on baseball in general and pitching in particular. Two conversations helped. The first was with coach/Dad and the other, at his dad's suggestion, was a further talk with Peter Morgan.

His dad was mostly concerned with whether or not Mack really wanted to pitch. "I realize," he said, "that I've got two agendas going on here—of course, wanting the team to have a good season but more importantly, not wanting to pressure you into doing something you don't want to do." This was almost exactly what Mack wanted to hear—that pitching or not—was his decision. And he said so.

What he heard from Peter Morgan was more practical pitching advice—everything from different grips on the ball to mental preparation before and during a game. "In a sense, pitching is a lot like shooting free throws in basketball. There is no one way to pitch. You discover what works for you. There are several common things to keep in mind, but you will need to figure out your own approach and then stick to what works. For example, and I'm sure you know this already, your windup should almost always look the same no matter what type of pitch you have decided to throw. Occasionally, it's okay to deviate if your purpose is to shake up the hitter when you suspect he thinks he knows what is coming. Again, like I said, you did well on Tuesday—especially for your first start. If you keep working on your game, I guarantee you will only get better."

"Yeah. Practice, practice, practice—like any sport you want to be good at."

"Well, that's right. And there's one more thing that I noticed in the Tuesday game. I know you were almost exclusively using your fastball. And that's okay for a while. But eventually, good hitters will catch on to your speed, so you need to find ways to vary that speed. You're a good hitter, Mack. What do you think about when you step into the batter's box?"

"You mean do I think or try to guess what the pitcher's going to throw?" Morgan nodded. "Actually, I try not to guess, especially when I've got two strikes. If I'm expecting a fastball and get an off-speed pitch instead, not only do I end up looking like a fool, I probably strike out as well. So I know better about anticipating too much, but I still find myself doing it anyway."

"Yes, and that's important. The best hitters try to clear their mind of guesses and allow their basic hand-eye coordination to adjust their swing in the moment. But oftentimes, depending on the count, the number of outs, and the number of men on base and the game situation—who's ahead, who follows in the lineup, what experience you've had with a pitcher in the past, etc.—then nine times out of ten, a hitter might think he can make an accurate guess. So if a hitter is thinking we are likely going to throw him a fastball, if possible, we pitchers will try to serve that batter what he is not expecting.

"As a pitcher, learn to think like a hitter. Given the situation, what might the hitter be expecting? What do you know about his strengths and weaknesses? Is he a good fastball hitter? Does he often swing at balls out of the strike zone? Has he shown he can hit a curveball? How about a preference for high pitches as opposed to low ones? Then of course, there are times when he is expecting a certain pitch and you throw it anyway because—"

"Because it's my best pitch?"

"Right. Let's say that your best pitch is your fastball, which it is for most young guys. And let's say the batter likes fastballs. And let's say the count is 2–2, last of the ninth. You're up by a run and there are two runners on. What do you throw? There is no right or wrong answer, at least not an obvious one. Give it a shot."

"Okay, if I felt confident about it, I'd try to throw a pitch that looked like a fastball but wasn't—like a slider or a screwball, if I had one."

"And if?"

"You mean if I wasn't that confident about something off speed?" Morgan nodded. "Then I'd go with the pitch I was most confident in, even if he was expecting it." Morgan nodded again.

"And if he goes ahead and hits it out of the park?"

"Then I put it behind me and get ready to face the next hitter."

"Exactly."

*****

Perhaps it was the newly established routine that made a difference. Deciding that he wanted to pitch coupled with the confidence of his teammates made focusing on each hitter that much easier. Of course, he wasn't 100 percent successful. He lost focus sometimes. Even with Stan's help behind the plate, he made mistakes and threw the wrong pitch to the wrong spot. Good hitters sometimes even hit his best pitches thrown in exactly the place he intended to throw them. But that's baseball! One of the harder things <u>was</u> to put his mistakes or his opponents' good hits behind him and move quickly on to the next challenge. Nevertheless, with consistent defensive and offensive support from the rest of the team and once Softstuff returned, a two-person pitching rotation, the YJs began to look like a different team.

Mack knew he could now count on pitching at least once a week. He continued to work on improving his control, particularly of his off-speed pitches. Over those midseason weeks, pitching once and often twice, his confidence grew and with it his effectiveness in wins over the Black Knights, the Grand Salamis, Charlie's Angels, and the Callapa Bay Oysters. Through the month of June, after that first loss to the Grand Ss, a six-game winning streak brought the YJs close to a first-place tie with the First Responders. They had now entered the last two weeks of the season and the emerging possibility of that three-game series with the Lincoln High School team had become a reality.

It is time to have another talk with Johnny or it will be too late. Mack and Johnny had continued their extra pitch-and-catch practice. This gave Mack some of the time he needed to get ready for his pitching assignments. But Mack's less-than-subtle agenda and an equally important reason to him was to strengthen Johnny's confidence and make sure that he was ready to make his own pitching debut when the time came, *whenever that was.*

Mack tried to hold down his enthusiasm for Johnny's ability since John Raymond had made it quite clear that he did not want to be pressured. For his part, Johnny seemed content to carry on as usual. Meanwhile, the Johnny Rainbow—hecklers continued to gather at YJ games. They weren't there every game but almost always on Saturdays. Johnny pretended like it didn't bother him, but now that he knew him that much better, Mack could tell there was still an impact—a tightening of the muscles, a nervous eye tic, a deep breath when there was no other reason for stress, an overly enthusiastic swinging of three bats in the on-deck circle. And the rest of the team was affected as well. Many a hostile glare settled on that pocket of fans behind the opposing teams' dugout. Mack lived in some fear that Johnny would suddenly decide that baseball wasn't fun anymore and walk away.

On Sunday, July 1, Johnny and Mack's Sunday practice had come to an end. The July Fourth holiday break was ahead, and there were two more scheduled games before the break, then two more and a bye ahead of the YJs after the fourth. Mack figured they needed to win at least three of those four games if they were going to finish in first place. Moreover, if Johnny could be convinced, in order to establish some in game confidence, he would need to pitch in at least one if not two games before the high school series. Time was running out. From Mack's perspective behind or beside the plate, there was nothing wrong with Johnny's pitching. He was ready. But it did not look like he believed that or if so he sure wasn't saying as much.

"Johnny, can we talk?" Mack finally asked as they prepared to go their separate ways again. "How about an ice cream?"

"I thought I told you I don't particularly like ice cream."

"Oh, right. Then a wonderful cup of hot chocolate."

"It's too hot for that."

"Come on. Let's go to the Spoon. Surely, you can find something on the menu. My treat."

"Look, Mack, I know what you're trying to do. And mostly, I appreciate it. But what the hell? The Rainbow guys are still at it, and I don't want to give them more ammunition. And we're winning anyway. The team doesn't need me on the mound."

"I get it. Just give me some time. Okay?"

Johnny finally nodded and agreed to follow Mack down to the Spoon. Five minutes later, they were sitting in the back corner booth. It was three in the afternoon on Sunday, and except for Susan, they were the only ones in the place. Johnny was sipping on a large iced mocha, which appeared to be at least half whipping cream. Mack toyed with the straw and long-handled spoon while occasionally using one or the other on a more than grande chocolate-peppermint milkshake.

"If you keep up with that diet, you're going to end up a fat ex-jock before you know it, ya know."

"Yeah, well, if you drink more than one of those things a day, you're not likely to lessen your stress levels anytime soon. There's enough caffeine in that to keep me awake for a week."

"So to each his own."

"And I guess that's applicable to more than one thing we've got to talk about. So go ahead. You first."

"No, you."

"At this rate, we'll never get anything worthwhile said."

"Maybe there is nothing worthwhile to say."

"I don't believe that and I don't think you do either. But since I called this meeting, I'll lead off. I've got three arguments in favor of you pitching and none of them have to do with how good you are."

Mack paused to make sure Johnny was listening. Johnny nodded but with a sigh and a look that communicated he expected to hear absolutely nothing new. "Maybe this will not be new to you, but bear with me all the way through, please." Again, Johnny nodded. "First, I appeal to you as a teammate. We need you, especially when we play two out of three with the high school. Let's say I pitch the Friday game and Softy pitches Saturday. What are the chances of us winning both? And if we lose one, even if we both manage to complete nine innings, neither of us will be ready for Sunday—at least I won't be. Or what if one of us needs a relief pitcher or if we get rained out and have to play a double header? Second, I think it's asking too much of anybody to pitch his first game under extra stress with no experience—like if you put off your debut until the high school series. And that means we need you to pitch at least one of the next three games."

"Mack, I—"

"Wait a minute or two. You'll have your chance. Three, I think you really do want to take on the Lincoln guys. This is your chance and likely, the only one you'll have. And I know this because I feel almost exactly the same way—for different reasons, yes. But still, I suspect you'll regret it if you don't give it a shot. Finally, and I've been giving this a lot of thought, I know that the Johnny Rainbow—shit still bothers you, even when you're trying to pretend it doesn't. I have a plan for that. No, listen. I'm not about to do anything without your buy-in. What if—"

CHAPTER 24

A Plan Comes to Life

Of course, it wasn't that easy. Nothing ever is, not when people are involved. That Sunday, Johnny said he would need some more time to think through Mack's proposal. Mack didn't hear from him until late Monday evening. When the text message came, it simply said, "Okay." *Well, then,* Mack thought, *some folks are in for a surprise or two.* And he finally was able to have that candid conversation with his dad.

Meanwhile, another full Tuesday hustling sodas, sundaes, and fancy coffee at the Spoon was followed by another pitching assignment against the Swedish Meatballs. Actually, the game started with Softstuff on the hill. The YJs offense built a 7–2 lead going into the fifth inning. The Meatball rally started innocently enough. Softy struck out the first batter and got the second one on a high pop fly to shallow left that Georgeena chased down before almost colliding with Mack. With two out, the Meatball leadoff hitter worked Softy for a base on balls. The next hitter slapped a single to right. A double off the bat of the number three hitter cleared the bases followed by an error by Alford at third and yet another double to run the score to 7–6.

Coach/Dad called a time-out and after a brief meeting with Softy, signaled for Mack to pitch in relief. He threw about fifteen practice pitches. Sam Jackson joined him on the mound.

"I think," Sam said quietly, "that these guys will not be able to catch up with your fastball, especially after six innings of Softstuff—no pun intended."

"Sounds good. Same signs. A closed fist always goes back to the fastball?"

Sam nodded. "Remember, there are two outs," he said, then walked back and took his spot behind the plate.

"Play ball!" stated the ump with the usual unnecessary vigor.

Mack took his stretch, looked over his shoulder at the guy on second, and threw his first pitch—a fastball—over the heart of the plate. And the hitter had no trouble catching up with the speed. He connected solidly, sent a rising line drive well over Larry Chen's head, and headed for the right center field fence. Mack, stunned for a moment, was barely aware of the runner on second touching the third-base sack and heading home. His eyes were focused on the ball when he saw Johnny in an all-out sprint from his center-field position, closing on both the ball and the fence. Would it clear the fence for a home run? Would he get there in time? Would he hurt himself trying to catch the uncatchable? Go, Johnny, go.

At the last possible second, Johnny turned back toward the field, stopped, jumped with his glove about a foot over the eight-foot-high wall, and appeared to snare the ball just before it could disappear over the fence. He came to rest with his back to the base of the fence wall, reached his hand in his glove, and held up the ball for all to see. *It really was an amazing catch,* easily the best Mack had seen all year. And Johnny wasn't hurt. He leapt to his feet and came running in toward the dugout. Mack met him with a high five.

"So you don't want me in center field. Are you sure?" He grinned.

"Hey, man. You can play center as often as you want—when I'm pitching." And he grinned back.

Sam joined them on the dugout bench. "Great catch, Johnny. My bad, Mack. I guess that guy could catch up with your fastball. Though I think he just got lucky."

"About gave me a heart attack," said Mack. "Let's get some more runs!" he yelled to the rest of the bench. Then he offered more quietly, "Just in case it wasn't luck."

For those last three innings, the YJs didn't produce any more runs for Mack. But except for a couple of scattered singles, Mack's pitching also kept the other team in check, including a second confrontation with the player whose drive had chased Johnny almost over the fence in the sixth. This time, on a 2–2 count with a runner on second in the last of the ninth, Mack struck him out with a low, outside curveball. The 7–6 score became the final.

*****

They had entered the season's home stretch, even up in the loss column with the Black Knights, who had also come on strong at the end of the season and one full game up on the First Responders. The YJs played the Callapa Bay Oysters on Saturday, followed by a head-to-head game with the Knights, a bye and the season ender against the Grand Salamis. The Knights were also set to play the Responders in what might prove to be the critical last game of the regular schedule. But if the YJs could win out, they would finish in first place and wouldn't have to worry about the others. Next would be the three-game series with the high school, if, if, if.

The only missing factor, as far as Mack was concerned, was working Johnny Raymond into the pitching rotation. Step one had been the building of Johnny's confidence during their one-on-ones. Step two was to bring the team on board. Wednesday's practice helped that cause. Mack convinced his dad to turn the usual informal batting-and-fielding workout into a more formal and competitive three-inning game with him pitching for one side and Johnny for the other. The stated purpose was to prepare the team to face the kind of high school pitching they would encounter if they made it to the series. The underlying rationale was to further build Johnny's confidence as well as the team's confidence in Johnny's pitching.

Intentionally, the batting lineup that faced Johnny was mostly the YJ starters. Nine outs later for both sides and there were no doubters left. Most of the YJ hitters had barely managed to touch the ball. Against Johnny, Mack reached base on a ground ball single but got no further.

Coach/Dad was impressed. "Johnny, you start Saturday," he said. "Can everyone be here about thirty minutes early? There's some team strategy that we all need to be on board with before we take the field."

"Everyone's here now," said Wexler. "What's up?"

"I'm going to leave that up to Mack and Johnny." Of course, everyone turned to look at both of them. Mack shrugged, but he had been half expecting the question.

"We have to get the details worked out first," he said. "Don't worry. We're not going to ask you to do anything too strange. Just put this all down to teenage angst. I'm not trying to look too far ahead, but in case you don't know this already, Johnny and I really, really want to be ready for the high school. Nuff said."

*****

Johnny Raymond's pitching debut in Columbia City's Commercial Baseball League came on the first Saturday of July against the Callapa Bay Oysters. The weather cooperated fully—bright sun, a few scattered clouds, and 75 degrees. The YJs were the visitors and determined to present their pitcher with a lead. That, they did. Chen, hitting leadoff since Johnny was on the hill, slapped a single to left. On a full count, Mack doubled into the right-center gap, scoring Larry. Al Alford's sharp single up the middle sent Mack to third. It was hit too hard for him to score. Two outs later, Mack was wishing he had tried anyway. But with runners on third and second, after Alford had taken second on a fielder's choice, Geena Daniels came through with another single through the right side. Both runners were off with the crack of the bat and two out. They scored easily. The YJs led 3–0 when Josh Kelsey struck out to end the top half of the inning.

Taking his warm-up pitches before the bottom half, Johnny appeared focused but loose. *I'm probably more nervous than he is,* thought Mack. "Let's get this show on the road!" *Did I say that out loud? Oops.* "Johnny, be good," he finished—definitely out loud—as Sam's throw went quickly to Larry Chen at second and around the horn to Alford at third. Al trotted to the mound and placed the ball in Johnny's glove. He said something inaudible, Johnny glanced briefly toward Mack, and Mack raised his hand in a thumbs-up gesture, repeating his statement, "Johnny, be good!" Johnny nodded and took his spot on the pitcher's rubber. He nodded once to Sam squatting in the catcher's position, wound up, and threw his fastball near the middle of the plate for strike one. He then proceeded to throw eight straight balls. Sam called time and he and all the infielders gathered in a circle around Johnny. Johnny pounded his glove in frustration. He was obviously upset with himself.

"Hey, man, relax," said big Al Alford. "This is not the World Series."

"We're behind you," said Larry Chen.

"Don't try to strike everyone out" were Coach/Dad's words.

"We've got your back," added Mack.

And from Sam the catcher, "Take your time, John. You're rushing your pitches a little bit. When you take your stretch, also take a deep breath, then focus on your target. Throw strikes. You'll be fine."

Before breaking up the huddle, Mack reached over and patted Johnny on the back with his glove, saying, "You're the man, Johnny. You're the man." After they all jogged back to their positions, the supportive chatter continued from all over the diamond, "You're the man, John. You're the man."

Whether it was the sense that they were indeed all behind him or whether he used the break well to relax and focus (or both), Johnny found his rhythm. He struck out the three and four CBO hitters. On a 2–2 count, the number five batter did manage to lift a short fly just beyond Larry Chen's reach for a scratch single, which did score the runner from second. With the YJ lead now 3–1, Mack watched Johnny closely as he faced the next hitter. *Don't let one lucky hit upset you, my man,* he thought. It didn't. He retired the third out on a routine fly ball to Georgeena in left. For the rest of those first three innings, Johnny was unhittable.

The old chant started when he took the mound to face the Oysters in the bottom half of the fourth—the singsong, high-treble sound of "Johnny Rainbow. Johnny Rainbow." Mack and Johnny exchanged glances and nods. Mack looked toward the team bench and nodded twice. The YJ subs for the day unobtrusively made their way out of the dugout. Johnny continued his warm-up throws. The chanting continued. At Mack's signal, everyone but Johnny and catcher Sam ran quickly toward the CBO dugout side of the field and gathered at the fence line as close to the chanters as they could get and began their own chant—a very different-sounding version of "Johnny! Rainbow! Johnny! Rainbow" with a rap beat sound provided by Al and Stan.

And they were not alone. The glorious baseball day—weather wise—had brought out a seemingly spontaneous and much larger crowd than usual. Among them, there was a group of Lincoln students—Katy, Tad, several other athletes, male and female, plus a bunch of younger people Mack couldn't place but who looked familiar. The YJ bench players took their place standing in front of the stands, chanting but also as close to in the face of the provocateurs as they could get. And all of them joined the YJs team chant, "Johnny! Rainbow! Johnny! Rainbow! Go, Johnny, go!" For their part, the CBO team was obviously mystified. The only person who actually sounded upset was the umpire who kept trying to get everyone's attention. "Play ball! Play ball!" he yelled to no avail for a couple of minutes.

The YJ defensive team returned to their positions, but for quite some time, the chanting did not stop. Johnny smiled and Johnny pitched. Later in the game, someone attempted to raise the old singsong chant once again, but without much help from the YJs in the field, the new chant easily drowned out the old. The beat went on.

Mack should have been happy. His plan had worked and would probably work again, if needed. Johnny had pitched well, and the YJs had won the game easily, 7–1. But for Mack, there was an unexpected problem. While standing near the fence to join the team chant back in the fourth inning, he had seen three people in the stands that he was not expecting at all, especially not together. Seated in the middle of what Mack referred to as the singsongers were Darrel Coffin and Mark Wenger and between them, Elana Loving.

CHAPTER 25

Painful Truths

"Hi, Elana. This is Mack. Can we talk?"

"Yeah, sure. Whacha want to talk about?"

"You. Me. Us. I know I've been kind of busy. But I have meant to get in touch. You know, well, other things came up and I wasn't sure how you felt. And suddenly, school was out and we weren't like seeing each other. And there was prom night and the fight. And—"

"Look, Mr. Cool Guy, is this about the game today or not?"

"What about the game?"

"You know what about the game? I know you saw me."

"Okay, that's a part of it, I guess. I saw you and I saw who you were with."

"So?"

"Elana, I know I got no claim on you. You can be with whomever you want to. That's your business. But why Coffin? And why at my baseball game?"

"I wasn't aware it was YOUR baseball game. I thought baseball was a team sport, and anybody who wants to watch a game can. Anyways, I don't owe you an explanation, but if you want to know, I was there because Darrel invited me. He likes me. He wants to spend time with me."

"So this has nothing to do with me and Johnny."

"Right. The world does not revolve around you and your boyfriends."

Whoa, she's mad. Guess I can't blame her for that. Is there a way to get around this? Do I need to defend myself? Do I really want to? Do I really want to spend more time with her? Let's try the old reflection technique.

"You sound angry."

"Damn right, I'm angry. For a while there, I thought we had a good thing going, then you hurt yourself and ruin our first real date, then there's prom and along comes Johnny and you get in a fight with Darrel, and he gets kicked out of school. And you make out with me when you feel like it and dump me when you feel like it. I don't hear from you for weeks, then you see me out with a couple of friends and suddenly, I'm important enough to get in touch with again. What's that about, huh?"

Okay, she's right and she's not. And it's not that she was out with a couple of friends. It's who those "friends" are. And why, right? What are you trying to convince yourself about, Mack?

"Look, Elana, you are partly right. I don't like your choice of friends, but that really isn't my business. I never met either Coffin or Wenger until the prom fight. Apparently, you did know them and can hang out with them if you want. But I don't have to like it. I don't like them and no doubt the feeling is mutual. That's all, except I really did want to get together with you in spite of them. I don't know if I want to be your boyfriend, but I know I don't want to leave things hanging. And I'm sorry that I didn't call you sooner. I'll understand if you don't want to have anything to do with me, but if you do or aren't sure, can we please get together and talk? I really hate trying to deal with important stuff over the phone." There was a lengthy silence, but Mack could hear Elana breathing, so he knew she was still there. "Well," he added.

"Okay," she said with a sigh. "I've got my sister's car for the weekend. I'll pick you up. Sunday around eight?"

"Yeah. That'll work okay. See you then." *Geesh, I wonder why so late and why she wants to drive*, he thought.

*****

Sunday was another one of those beautiful Columbia City mid-summer days—pleasantly hot most of the day but cooling down with an evening breeze off the ocean by the time Elana arrived at Mack's place. She was driving her sister's old Buick convertible. The top was down, and Mack could hear the thump of the bass from the sound system before she pulled to a stop. For a moment, he wondered what mood she would be in and whether getting into a car with her was such a good idea. Once again, he realized how little he really knew about her. He paused. The situation seemed to call for it, so he placed his hand on the front door window ledge and literally leapt into the passenger seat. Elana pushed her foot to the floor, and with a squeal from the tires, they were off.

She glanced at him. "Wow, that was an impressive vault."

He glanced back. "That was an impressive acceleration. Nice wheels."

"Yeah, they are. I'm trying to convince my sister to sell it to me before she heads back to California."

Without looking very carefully, Elana turned a corner, narrowly missing a parked car, and stepped on the gas again. It was only a quiet neighborhood street, but she was well above the posted thirty-miles-per-hour speed limit.

"We in a hurry to get where we're going?"

"Why? Am I scaring you?"

"No, just your driving."

"Well, if you must know, I'm pretty sure that Chevy behind us a couple of blocks belongs to Darrel. I'm putting some distance between us." And with that, she whipped the steering wheel sharply to the left into a midblock alleyway, sped to the far end, and parked quickly in front of someone's garage.

"That should do it. To be sure, we'll wait a few minutes, then double back." *Whew!* he thought.

"So how are you, Mack?"

"Uh, fine or I was. Do you always drive like that?"

"Only when I need to get away from someone I don't especially want to see at the moment."

"So that was Coffin following us. Are you dating him now?"

"Can we not talk about that right now? At least until we get where we're going."

"And where would that be?"

"Let it be my surprise."

With that, she leaned over and pecked him on the cheek, then sat back with her back to the car door. She ruffled her hair with her fingers like one sometimes does after a drive in the open air. She stretched out her bare legs, her skirt inched up to mid thigh while she continued to glance up and down the alleyway. Whatever she was intending, Mack found her gestures, her slightly flushed appearance, the way her body seemed primed for immediate action impossible to interpret. She seemed—*what*—*dangerous, seductive, provocative, a little crazy, maybe all four plus.*

Mack had to admit to himself: There was a kind of electricity between them. He was turned on and repulsed by her at the same time. How could that be? *Whatever else,* she was certainly desirable. But then they had been down that road before and it hadn't turned out so well. And here they were, parked in some stranger's driveway, fleeing from a guy who was what if not her new boyfriend and who had every reason not to like Francis McKyer very well. What would happen if he spotted them again? Or maybe this whole thing was a plot devised by Coffin and Elana. Eventually, would she drive to some godforsaken place where the fight would continue?

Even though the house they were parked behind looked dark from where the car was, how would they explain themselves if someone decided to confront them? In an open convertible in a strange neighborhood, Mack felt exposed and vulnerable. What were they doing there—really? Both of them kept glancing around, up and down the alleyway, listening all the while for the sound of an approaching engine. A few minutes passed. They talked about a few superficial things. How was the summer going? How was work? How was baseball? Did she miss school? They listened—half an ear to each other, half to the outside world. Except for a brief interchange about the coming football season, they stayed away from anything related to prom night and its aftermath.

The sky was beginning to darken when Elana finally suggested that hopefully the coast was clear. She turned on the ignition and slowly drove toward the end of the alley. They then made their way back through the quiet neighborhood to a major four-lane avenue. Elana turned left, in the opposite direction from which they had originally headed. Traffic was brisk, and before long, they seemed lost amid other anonymous vehicles. They were both breathing more easily. Or so it seemed.

"Unless he's planted one of those thingamajiggers on my sister's car, I think we're free and clear. You sit back and relax."

About twenty minutes later, they had left most of the lights of the city and Elana turned onto a two-lane road, which appeared to be heading west and north. On both sides of the road for as far as Mack could see, there was nothing but evergreen forest. "Don't worry," Elana said. "I know where I'm going." Another two turns—the last one onto a rough gravel road—and a mile or so later, she pulled off into a small, rather primitive parking area. They were on a bluff, looking straight out toward the sea. Elana turned off the motor.

The sun was almost ready to disappear over a far-off mountain range. The sky was a deep orange and gold fading to purple. Far to their right, they could see a few lights twinkling from a small town. Otherwise, the area seemed deserted. Mack attempted to train his ear to any strange sounds that would indicate otherwise. He heard nothing but the piping of a few birds and the crash of the waves far below. They got out of the car. In the increasingly dim light, they walked close to the edge of the bluff and wandered out onto a large flat stone shelf stretched out over the cliff edge like a pier to nowhere. Still, it seemed solid enough. With no spoken plan, they sat side by side with backs to the parking area, looking out toward the sunset.

"How did you find this place?"

"No mystery. My aunt lives in Bakersville—those lights that you can see over there. We used to visit them when my cousins were little, and sometimes we'd hike up this way. I love the ocean, especially at sunset. I guess this is my favorite place in the world."

Mack relaxed for the first time in the last rather frenetic hour. It would be so easy to get lost in the romance of the moment and to forget the other things on his mind.

"Thanks for showing it to me," he said. And after a minute or so of silence, he said, "I don't want to spoil things, but I do want to talk about, you know, stuff. We said—a long time ago, ages it seems—that we would always speak truth to one another." He held up his hand to stop her from the interruption that he saw emerging on her tongue. "I know, I know. It's been more my fault than yours. I just haven't known how to handle things, so I've taken the easy way out and thrown myself into other stuff so I wouldn't have to think about you and me. And that's not been fair to you. I like you. I mean I hope you know that. Maybe I like you too much. And I'm not ready for any—"

"Mack, stop." And she leaned against him, put her arms around his neck, and kissed him passionately.

He felt his body briefly respond, then broke away from her a bit and said, "I thought you said stop."

"Not stop this, stupid," she said and kissed him again. And for the next few minutes, there was not much stopping. As the sun slowly disappeared over the horizon, Elana finally did stop and said, "This rock makes for a very hard bed. Let's go back to the car." *Elana, the Queen of Innuendos*, he thought but walked back to the car with her, arm in arm.

Once there, Elana gave him a short lesson in how the front seats reclined so they were nearly flat, then she curled up next to him and said, "That's better." And for a while, they both seemed content with the quiet and the closeness. But they were teenagers, and there was this electricity between them. And soon, the passionate kissing had resumed. Breathing was heavy and bodies were intertwined. *Now or never*, thought Mack. *But what was now and what was never?*

He didn't push her away, exactly. But he sat up with his back to the car door, still—for a moment—playing with her hair, holding her hand, a bit more firmly than he had to.

"Elana, I don't want to stop, but I don't want to hurt you more than I have. Please. You were so angry with me an hour ago. And nothing's changed, except we've confirmed that we like each other enough to do this. Please, I need to know what's going on with you."

There was a long pause, then Elana also sat up and moved toward the driver's side of the car. Mack felt their sudden distance, and a strong part of him wanted to cross the widened gap between them. Were there words that would help? He couldn't find any.

At first, she didn't say anything either, and in the now nearly dark sky, Mack could barely see her face. But he could hear her, and she was crying, at first quietly but then with increasingly obvious sobs. Then Mack did move toward her and put his arm around her. At first, she half-heartedly attempted to push him away, but when the tears did not subside, she collapsed into his lap and for a while, there were no words needed. She cried. He held her. He felt some moisture in his own eyes but couldn't have said what that was about. It was Elana who broke the silence this time.

"I wanted you. I want you to want me. And you're so damn good. You don't want to take advantage of anybody. I want you to take advantage of me. Why did I go out with Darrel? Because he wants me. He wants to be with me all the time. And you don't. You've got sports and a job and a family that cares about you. You know what I got? Nothing and no one—not anyone who cares just about me." She stopped for a moment and then plunged ahead.

"And there's my stepdad—you know, Mr. I'm too-good-to-even-shake-hands-with stepdad. He cares about me so much that he sneaks into my room late at night and…and does what he does, the fucking son of a bitch. Yeah, <u>he</u> wants me all right, so you are so right to stay away from me. I'm used goods. That's for sure—"

"Elana, I… I—"

And the tears came again. Mack really had no words—no words that would comfort, no words that would make what he had heard go away, and no words of love or healing that he could offer. He was as much angry as anything. And how would that help? He had questions, of course, like hadn't she told her mother. But even as he asked them, he knew they did not have the power to change anything. What had happened had happened. You couldn't make it go away with a right answer when there was none to be had. She had tried, she said, in so many ways, but her mom hadn't wanted to listen. She hated them both. Mack had heard her say that once before and hadn't understood it then. Now he thought he understood, but saying that wouldn't help either. He tried to say he cared about her, but that wasn't enough and he knew it even as he said it.

"I've never told anyone except my mom about this. I need you to promise you won't say anything."

"If you need me to promise, I will. But Elana [he tried again], you know what you are describing is abuse, and if you report it, he would be in big trouble and you could be free of him."

"Yeah, right. And what would happen to me? Would anyone really believe me? My word against his. They would both hate me more than they already do. I'd be kicked out and on my own. How would I survive? No, I've just got to make it through the next year, then go somewhere far away."

"Elana, I... I—"

"Mack, it's okay. I wanted your love. I don't want your pity." He had heard that before. Elana fastened her seat belt, turned out of the parking area, and drove back toward the city. About halfway, Mack tried to hold her hand, but she withdrew it, saying, "Good drivers keep both hands on the wheel." Then she smiled and said again, "You're a good man, McKyer. I think we could have been good together—maybe someday."

CHAPTER 26

Interlude

The regular season of the Columbia City Commercial Baseball League was over. Mack thought he would never say this, but there it was—*the Lincoln High School Lions awaited them.* And he was psyched. Of course, there were other things going on in his life besides baseball but nothing he had any control over. School wouldn't be starting for another month and a half with football preseason two weeks earlier. He hadn't heard anything from Coach Smitson recently, but he felt like he had done what he could do and decisions were now in other hands.

Work was an up-and-down enterprise, but what work isn't? He still enjoyed being around Susan and Randal. They expected him—and their other employees—to do their jobs. But they were fair and flexible about schedules, and they always had spare time if I guy needed to talk to a nonparent adult. Of course, with Randal, the conversation would usually turn to baseball. The other student employees were interesting and mostly fun people. Even working with Isabel, Kerry's Ding-Ding, was okay, though she teased him more than he liked. Apparently, she didn't see why everyone else seemed to make a big deal out of Mack being an athlete and holding down a job at the same time. Ah, well, work was fine, even with the extra summer hours. And his bank account was growing. That was a good thing.

Mack hadn't thought much about what he called his social life over the past couple of months. The fiasco with Elana—he guessed that's what it was—was the only date he had had all summer. He hadn't seen or heard anything from Lisa since March. And the list of "possibles" that he kept in the back of his high school annual had gone untouched and mostly unseen, except in his fantasy life.

With his guy friends, besides the frequent workouts with Johnny, there had been a couple of early morning golf and tennis outings. He had also found time to join Nate Garvery and company at the community center basketball courts on the few rainy mornings he wasn't working. Finally, he had hung out at the beach, mostly throwing Frisbees or footballs or joining in some beach volleyball. Come to think of it, no wonder what *some people* said—and he thought of both Katy and Isabel here—he was *not* boring since all he seemed to care about was sports. *Well, crap, maybe they are right for them.* But it was still summer and summer in Mack's life meant baseball. And for the moment, that was enough.

With their differing baseball commitments, he and Red hadn't seen much of each other either. The last time they had hung out, Kerry had made it clear—probably unintentionally—that he didn't see the commercial baseball league as on the same level as the city high school teams. "I'm glad you're having fun playing this year, but if you guys make it to our series, I wouldn't get too excited. We beat the First Responders two in a row last year, 10–1 and 8–3 I think. Our pitching is just too good. And face it, Mack, most of your players—present company excepted—are pretty much over-the-hill." Then perhaps to soften it a bit, he added, "Oh, I'm sure you and maybe that high school coach who plays for you will get a couple of hits, but don't be too disappointed when the series doesn't go three games."

*****

For the three days prior to the start of the Lincoln versus Yellow Jacket series, there was little else to talk about in the McKyer household, especially between Mack and his dad. They discussed lineup options, batting-order adjustments, sign changes, strengths and weaknesses of the high school players, and more than anything, the

YJ pitching rotation. Mack's mom listened to most of this with polite nods of her head. Jana was not so inclined.

"Damn it," she finally exploded at dinner Thursday night, "all you guys ever talk about is baseball, baseball, baseball. It's like nothing anybody else around here does is important. Didya ever think someone else might have an interesting something going on in her life? Didya ever think someone who's about to spend her first year in high school might be interested in something else besides throwing and catching and hitting? But no, it's baseball, baseball, baseball. As a family, we don't even get to go on summer vacations like most of the world because two of us have to spend every other day playing a stupid game or talking about the one they just finished. And the only thing the rest of us can do is watch. Well, I sure as hell am not going to do any more watching. I'm… I'm… I'm goin' shopping instead."

"Watch the language, young lady," quipped the mom in the room, though she didn't seem to make her concern sound very serious, "there's no reason we can't both watch a ball game and go shopping."

Jana glared in response.

Dad followed up with "So I've been giving it more thought and I'm thinking we'll start Softstuff in the first game."

"Well, crap," said Jana and left the table. Two male shrugs followed, but they didn't move. Dessert was still to come.

"I don't know, Dad. Peter has the experience, but I think Johnny would make for a stronger start. And the high school won't be expecting him I don't think—unless they've been spying on us recently."

"There's no doubt about who has the stronger arm, but two things to think about. First, the high school players are used to hotshot, mostly fastball pitchers. Softy will keep them off balance, at least for a while, and we can hold you or Johnny in relief if they catch on to him. But second, not only does Softy have the experience, he's been the main guy for this team going back several years. He deserves the opportunity. And third, if we do lose that first game, we've got two strong young arms to throw at them."

"Maybe that'll work, but regardless—and I've been thinking about this almost as long as when I knew we had a shot at this thing—we've got to start Johnny in game two."

"I had been thinking the opposite, Mack. I'd thought it should be you in game two. I'm proud of you." Mack started to interrupt, but his dad cut him off. "No, really, I am. I know at the start of the summer, you weren't crazy about even playing with the Yellow Jackets at all. But you came along, maybe as much to please me as anything—which I don't feel that great about. But you proved you belonged, even before the accident happened and then that prom mess. I really thought we might have lost you there with the possible threat to your senior year football participation. That would have been understandable and okay with me. Really. Actually, lost is probably not the right word. I mean lost in the sense that you would have limited attention to focus on our small-time baseball team."

Again, Mack started to interrupt with a disclaimer. Dad talked over him, "But you kept with it. And I'm especially proud of how you have worked with Johnny in spite of his, you know, his orientation."

"Dad, you're embarrassing me. His orientation had nothing to do with it. I did what I did because I love baseball and because I like Johnny. He's become my friend. And I want him to start that second game for basically the same reason you want Softy to start the first one. Because he deserves the chance to prove to some folks that he is a player and a damn good one. And really, it's all related: Johnny as a ballplayer and a friend, the prom business, and the way he was and is treated by a bunch of idiots that don't understand and aren't interested in trying. Yeah, as you know, I've got some things to prove, too, but his are more important."

"I get it, son. I don't know if you have any evening plans. Just get a good night's sleep. If you aren't pitching, we'll need a wide-awake shortstop tomorrow as well."

"I'm going to slide over to Kerry's for a bit. I want to see if I can make him a little more anxious. He was far too confident the last time we talked."

"Just don't share our strategy with him."

"Not to worry."

*****

The day of game one dawned with a heavy fog covering most of the city. The game was scheduled for 7:00 p.m. at the high school field. Mack hadn't slept that well, but by 9:00 a.m., he was up and staring glumly at the cloud cover out the back window. His mom had taken the day off and was futzing around the kitchen, making crepes of all things. She glanced at him with his nose pressed against the window.

"Not to worry," she said. "This'll burn off before noon."

"If you say so," he responded. "All I can say is you better be right."

"You know, this is my first July in Columbia City. But people, including all the church people, tell me all the time the summer fog comes inland from the sea at night but always burns off, so there. I've got it on high authority."

"Okay then. That's settled. What's for brunch?" Jana strode in as he asked.

"French crepes à la McKyer," she said, "though I don't know why you deserve them."

"Hey, I've been up a whole five minutes and I haven't talked about baseball yet."

"Whoopee doodle." Then he really couldn't help himself.

"So let me get your true opinion, o wise sister. Do you think Carlisle Williamson can hit my curveball?"

"Who's Carlisle Williams?" she asked and then she got it. "Why you, you baseball nut. And whoever he is, I hope he hits it out of the park!" And she stomped off, yelling, "Tell me when the crepes are done."

After a full brunch of crepes, fruit, some side-meat choices, and only four references to baseball—mostly made innocently by Dad—Mack tried to do some reading. His plan was to then take a long nap before dinner at five. The reading was good for about three hours. But when he lay down, he couldn't sleep. The butterflies of anxiety were fluttering in his gut, and he needed to do something. Mom's weather prediction was spot on. It was now sunny and about 72 degrees. The only problem, baseball wise, was a brisk and gusty wind blowing from the northwest. Mack decided to take the dog for a walk. It was less than a mile to the park, and he figured there and back again would be about right and maybe, just maybe that would help settle his stomach.

The wind didn't seem to bother Patches much. In fact, she seemed much more interested in running than Mack did and not at all ready to go back home once they got to the main park entrance. So he turned in toward an area he knew he could let her off leash for a good run on her own. There would be an interesting result attached to that decision, though he didn't know it at the time.

Mack sat on a park bench—in fact, the same one he and Katy had shared a couple of months earlier. *So much has happened since the end of the basketball season*, he thought. And before long, he was half dozing as he went over the past little while in his head—especially the high school baseball tryouts, his decision to cut classes, the hurt and anger, the meetings in the principal and vice principal's offices, the abuses suffered by Johnny "Rainbow" Raymond and Elana Loving, the injustices, and the opportunities to right them. He was lost there for a while when suddenly, a young woman's voice penetrated his consciousness. She was definitely invading his personal space, standing right in front of him. The sun was at her back and in his eyes, so he couldn't see much of anything but a glare. She appeared to be holding a dog, which appeared to be Patches—was Patches.

And she was saying, with some aggravation in her voice, "Is this your dog?"

What else could he say? "Yeah, where did you find her?" Clearly, this was not enough of a response for this girl/woman.

"Are you sure? You're looking like you're from another planet or at least not very at home in this one. She's not exactly acting like she knows you. The only reason I'm asking is because you are the only person I see around here with a dog leash beside you and no dog."

Mack was most assuredly awake at this point, and he was beginning to be a little irritated with the girl's attitude as well as feeling a bit of guilt for not watching the dog more closely. "Of course, she's my dog. Thank you for finding her. She can't exactly come to me while you're holding her."

"Oh, right," she said and put Patches on the ground a few feet away.

Experiencing freedom once more, Patches took off at a run toward the bordering forest. Frequently stopping for a sniff, the dog appeared to be in a search for the source of some kind of odor. Fortunately for Mack (since the girl/woman was obviously experiencing further doubts about dog and ownership), Patches (having thoroughly sniffed the designated area of interest) came loping back when Mack stood up and called her about four times. He then returned to his spot on the bench. When Patches reached them, she ignored the woman and leapt with great confidence straight on to Mack's lap. Mack shrugged. "That's kind of how she is, likes to decide things in her own time." Then he added, for what reason, he wasn't sure, "Have a seat if you'd like."

She sat, which of course, gave Patches the further permission to move over to her lap. The girl/woman—obviously, Mack could not decide which fit best—then said the obvious, "I like your dog. Did I hear you call her Patches?"

It was one of those moments—reminiscent a bit of the first time he had really talked with Lisa or maybe Elana. Two minutes turned into twenty. She came to this park frequently, she said, to get away from home, get some exercise, enjoy the gardens, and the views of mountains and sea. She hedged when he asked her anything personal—where she lived, went to school, etc. But she was interested in his answers to her personal questions. Mack decided he would play things according to her undisclosed rules and avoided direct answers as well. It became a rather interesting fencing match, and he even said that at one point. She pretended not to know what he meant but rather abruptly handed Patches back to him, stood up, and said she needed to leave. "I like your dog and enjoyed talking with you. See ya around." And she was off. And he realized a few seconds later, she hadn't even told him her name. *Did I tell her mine?*

CHAPTER 27

The Series: Game 1

The walk home, the changing into uniform, gathering of baseball gear, and the short drive to the high school field felt a bit anticlimactic. He had anticipated these games for so long. And now suddenly, they were here. Today was here. And surprise, it was just another game. The weather, complete with sun and gusting winds, had continued the rest of the afternoon. The groundskeepers had been busy. The field was freshly lined and the grass about as short as it could be in the outfield. Like many high school diamonds, there was no grass on the infield and on occasion, the windy conditions stirred up small dirt devils—little mini tornados—which wandered their way back and forth before dying down in the grass.

The first player to arrive besides Mack and his dad was Peter Morgan. "Why don't you put some catching gear on and warm up Pete until Sam gets here?" suggested Coach/Dad.

"Sure. Does he know he's starting?"

"Yep."

For about ten minutes, Morgan loosened up and between throws, he and Mack chatted about the weather and about pitching.

"Does the weather bother you or do you not pay attention to it? I mean what about this wind?"

"Mostly, the latter of those two choices. Once I get on the mound, like I've said to you before, I try to stay as focused as possible on each batter." Slow curveball. "And if I do consider the weather, it has to do with how I can use it to advantage. For example, is the field laid out so that the sun is shining in a player's eyes or creating shadows that might hide the ball some?" Slower curveball. "Or with this wind, will the pitches I throw have more or less movement—even a little?" Slower still, split-finger knuckleball with downward movement. "The sun means we're all going to sweat more. Does a little sweat on the baseball that I don't wipe off—we used to call that a spitball for obvious reasons—make a pitch slide more in one direction or another?" Slider.

"So"—Mack grinned—"we'll see what happens on a day like today, complete with wind, sweat, and sun in the eyes."

"Yes, we will. I'm looking forward to it!"

By the time Sam Jackson arrived, Mack was getting a taste of how many different kinds of changes of pace and breaking balls Softstuff had in his repertoire. "I'm glad I don't have to face you. I don't know how some of those guys manage to connect as solidly as they do. Here ya go, Sam. He's looking about as sharp as I've seen all summer."

Mack now glanced around the field. Focused on the pitching warm-up, he hadn't noticed that most everyone from both teams was present and in various stages of pregame preparation. The high school team was in the middle of infield practice. Coach Hanson was expertly knocking ground balls to each of the infielders in turn. Mack tried to ignore his antipathy toward the high school coach, but it was difficult.

He watched, however, with some appreciation as his high school friends, acquaintances, and former teammates whipped the ball around the diamond. There was the catcher, Amos Jenkins—a football tight end, one of two directing things from behind the plate. Two infielders were warming up at each position. Kerry was one of those at his usual second-base spot. J. J. Jackson and Carlisle Williamson were taking turns receiving throws and handling grounders at first base.

Mack did not know DeQuan Ellis or Terry Clayton, who were taking turns at short and third—only their names. Partly because of his own position at short, he was more interested in evaluating them as well as Ryan Ostler, the regular high school third baseman who was a friend. All seemed to know what they were doing. On a sharp ground ball to his left, Ellis moved catlike to glove the ball, flipped it smoothly to Red at second, and Red made the pivot and threw a seed to J. J. at first—most likely a double play if it had unfolded that way during a game. The next moment, Ostler smoothly bare-handed a slow roller to third and threw accurately to first. Without looking at the lineup card Hanson submitted, it was impossible to know who would start.

Of the six guys chasing down outfield flies, there were at least two guys Mack knew well: Fred "The Fly" Waters (a wide-receiver in football) and Lamont Stevens (a key defensive back in football and a star forward on the basketball team). Again, it was impossible to know who the starters would be.

Mack didn't personally know either of the two pitchers warming up on the sideline and asked Johnny about them—Louis Jones, throwing right-handed, looked about as fast or faster than anyone Mack had seen in the commercial league. He was throwing harder than Jake Levinsky, a left hander, who had a herky-jerky motion reminiscent of the old LA Dodger pitcher, Clayton Kershaw. Mack's only thought there was to hope Levinsky wasn't as difficult to hit as Kershaw—unlikely that.

He turned away from the action on the field and focused on his own warm-ups. He did heave a sigh. It was a kind of what-if moment. But with a relief, regrets he had stored up for the first half of the summer mostly disappeared. Those guys—there sure were a lot of them—were not the enemy any longer. But he was a competitor and he wanted, about as much as he had ever wanted anything, to beat them—to show anyone watching that he belonged on the same field.

Maybe Mack should have been nervous when it was the YJ's turn to take the field, but he wasn't—not much anyway. The butterflies disappeared with the first ground ball hit his way. Yeah, he suspected that the high school team and coaches would be watching him more closely or maybe not—maybe that was just his pride speaking. But so what? He could make six errors or strike out three times. So what? *Before long, I'm going to be sounding like my sister, "It's just a baseball game!""* he thought.

"Play ball!"

And what a game it was. For the first several innings, both pitchers were in charge—Jake Levinsky for the Lincoln Lions and especially Softstuff Morgan for the Yellow Jackets. In some ways, Levinsky was a young Morgan. He had excellent control, was hitting the corners with his slider, and much of the time, kept the YJs off balance with a variety of soft curves and changeups. He wasn't, however, good enough to keep them off the bases. The YJs used a variety of hustle plays, mostly bunts, hit-and-runs, steals, sac flies, and one timely home run from Sam Jackson to build a 4–0 lead. Johnny had a bunt single, two steals, and scored on Mack's single in the third and Sam's home run in the top half of the fifth. *So much for Kerry's prediction.*

For those first innings, every one of the high school hitters appeared to be trying, with no success, to knock the ball out of the park. When the Lions hadn't cut into the YJ lead through five in the last half of the sixth, Hanson made several lineup changes. It had been clear to Mack and to anyone who followed the high school team regularly that Hanson had not started his first team players. Perhaps it was because he wanted to give more opportunities to the younger backup guys who would be likely starters the following season. Or maybe he didn't think the YJs would offer strong competition. Maybe he and the team he started were overconfident. And maybe it was a bit of all those factors. In any case, when the Lions' first team lineup came in as pinch hitters or took the field in the seventh, a clear change in attitude was obvious.

Gone was the loose playfulness the high school team had demonstrated during warm-ups and the first part of the game. There were no grins, only grim determination on the faces of the high school hitters as they came to the plate. And the baseball Lions did begin to hit. The bottom of the eighth was crucial. With the score 4–2 YJs, the Lions filled the bases with one out on a double, an infield error, and a walk. Karl McKyer, who was playing first, called a time-out and the whole infield gathered around Softstuff Morgan. The typical dialogue of such times ensued.

"How you feeling, Peter—tired?"

"A little, but I think I've got enough in the tank."

"Dad, Coach, I can relieve if you need me to."

"Your call, Karl."

"We'll stay with Softy."

The next high school hitter was Mack's good friend, Lamont Stevens. He hadn't started the game and was one of those who had subbed in. This was his first at bat. Mack stayed behind the others long enough to say, "Peter, I don't know for sure what kind of hitter Lamont is, but he is a very good athlete, so I'm guessing he's at least pretty good. Be careful. Probably keep the ball low and maybe we can get a double play and get you out of this unscathed."

Morgan nodded, then laughed. "Hey, kid, thanks. I'll give it my best. And if he hits it, he hits it. And if we're lucky, he'll hit it right to you."

Mack wasn't sure if it was Lamont or Softstuff who worked the count full. He used to think that working the count was the hitter's thing, but since becoming something of a pitcher, he had begun to think the opposite. Anyway, unless there's a foul ball, when the count reaches 3–2, it can't go any further. Someone is about to win and someone about to lose. Peter Morgan did not want to give in to this high school hitter, so he threw what he thought was his best pitch, a slow curve that was meant to drop over the low, outside corner of the plate.

Somehow, Lamont Stevens had figured this out or at least it looked like he had. Instead of trying to pull the ball, he stepped almost across the plate, made good contact, and drove the ball on a line straight toward Stan Borison in right field. Stan took one mistaken step in, then turned and sprinted toward the wall, but he might as well have walked. The ball sailed up and out, riding that gusting wind, over the fence, a grand slam home run, and now a 6–4 lead for the high school Lions. Everyone on the high school bench and on their side of the stands was on their feet yelling and chanting, "Lamont. Stamp, stamp, stamp. Lamont, etc." In an uncharacteristic gesture, Peter Morgan threw his glove on the ground and jumped on it before he realized he was pretty much looking like a fifty-year-old idiot. Then the umpire threw him a new ball, and he went back to work. The bases were empty, and he kept them that way.

But the damage was done, and when the YJs came in for the top half of the ninth, they trailed by two. And Hanson brought in his closer, Jason Phelps. Mack had no trouble recognizing him—the high school batting practice pitcher who had attempted, with some success, to show him up during the early spring tryouts. It was the top of the YJ order, so Johnny was the first batter to step in. And two things happened in quick order. For the first time all day, the Johnny Rainbow—chant lifted its ugly tones from somewhere behind the high school dugout. Then on the first pitch, Phelps threw a high inside fastball that Johnny tried to duck. It caught him on the shoulder. Several of the YJs ran toward the plate to make sure Johnny was okay. He shrugged them off and trotted to first, looking at the pitcher the whole way. Phelps did not turn away. He didn't say anything, though his expressions seem to suggest he had no regrets and would likely throw the same pitch again if he could.

Hanson called time and trotted out to the mound, perhaps with that very concern. No one could hear what was said, but a part of it was likely the message that their team was only up by two runs and more base runners was not a good option. Mack stepped in to face Jason Phelps. Johnny took a moderate leadoff first. Phelps ignored him. The first pitch was a high inside fastball, which Mack took for ball one. Mack stepped out of the box and glared at the pitcher. Jason grinned back. It was not a pleasant look for either of them. They stared at one another a little too long. This drew the automatic play ball from the umpire. Mack stepped back in and cocked his bat. Again, Johnny's leadoff first was modest, but as Jason took his stretch and went into his windup, Johnny was off. The second pitch was a curve over the outside edge for strike one, and Johnny slid into second without a throw. Amos Jenkins, now the catcher, called time and walked out for a brief chat with Jason.

Whatever he said, Jason appeared to pay closer attention to the base runner and was all business as he took the sign and threw another breaking pitch, which started out headed right at Mack before breaking sharply over the inside corner. Thinking it was another inside fastball, Mack had backed quickly away and felt a bit foolish when the pitch turned into a strike. *Now what will he throw? Two strikes. I've got to be ready for anything.* And he was, sort of. The pitch came in toward the outside corner but did not curve off the plate. Mack swung a bit late and sent a towering fly to right field. Johnny tagged up and strolled into third easily, but Mack was the first out of the inning.

A second fly ball off the bat of Alan Alford brought in Johnny with another run. Now the score was 6–5 with two outs, and Sam Jackson was the YJ's last hope. For a second or two, his long fly toward the left foul pole brought that hope alive to the YJ dugout. They all jumped to their feet and saw the ball swerve foul by a few feet. On a 3–2 count, Sam chased an outside curveball and missed it for strike three and the ball game. The high school team now held a 1–0 lead in the three-game series.

CHAPTER 28

The Series: Game II

To say that the first game loss was a disappointment to the Yellow Jackets would be an understatement. Lying in bed that night, Mack replayed his fly ball out in the ninth over and over again. He had not done his part and maybe that had been the difference. The next morning, Kerry dropped by. They watched some SportsCenter and played a couple of video games. Eventually, of course, the talk turned to the series.

"So you guys almost got us."

"Yeah, until Hanson finally put the first team in."

"So you noticed that."

"I wondered. At least I couldn't imagine why he didn't start his all-star second baseman."

"Ha. Ha. And things were still in doubt until Lamont hit that shot in the eighth."

"Are you gonna stick with your starters this next time around?"

"How do I know? That's up to Hanson. But if I had to guess I'd say yes. He hates to lose, and I don't think he's ready to trust some of next year's likely team. But what about you? Who you gonna start on the mound? Wasn't that Morgan guy your best pitcher?"

Mack fibbed a little bit. "Who knows for sure. That's up to the manager."

"Uh, the manager is your dad, Mack."

"Well, he doesn't tell me everything he's planning." Which was kinda the truth.

"I heard a rumor that your Johnny Rainbow has been doin' some pitching." Mack shrugged. "Might be a mistake to throw him out there. You know how some of the high school fans are."

"Yeah, I know, but not if you don't encourage them."

"Whoa, baby, don't lay that on me. If that chanting shit starts." Mack looked up quickly from the game monitor. "Yeah, I know about that. The word is out. Just tell your boy to ignore it."

"Easier said than done, my friend. How would you like it if you were the target?"

"Well, I wouldn't be, would I? 'Cause I don't hang with the gay crowd. Okay, then I need to get goin'. Got a few things to do before game time. See ya."

Mack murmured, "Yeah, see ya." Then he picked up his phone and made a few calls.

*****

On Saturday afternoon, the sun was still shinning. The wind had died down to a dull whisper since the day before. The temperature was about the same, but it felt 10 degrees warmer. The word was definitely out among the high school crowd, current students and former, and they showed up by the hundreds. Along with a fair representation of the other members of the commercial league a half hour before game time, the stands were nearly full and fans were lining the outfield. It was at least quadruple the number that had attended any previous YJ games to date. Perhaps it was his imagination, but Mack thought he heard some heightened crowd interest when Johnny Raymond went out to the bullpen mound to begin his pregame warm-ups.

Mack worried that Johnny would be psyched out by the large crowd. A couple of minutes before game time, Johnny came in from the bullpen and plopped down on the dugout bench next to Mack while they waited for the official announcements of the starting lineups.

"How ya doin'?"

"Okay, how about you?"

"You know what I mean. Just give me our thumbs-up signal if and when—"

"Will do. It still feels like special treatment to me, but if the team wants it, I'll take it if need be." Then he added, "My guys are here too."

"It's only special because you are and you deserve it. The team really wants you to know we're behind you. Okay?"

"Okay. And, Mack, you do not need to take care of me." Mack nodded, only a little embarrassed. "And not to change the subject," Johnny added, "but take a look in the grandstand behind home plate, about two-thirds of the way up—two guys in Lincoln Lion T-shirts, baseball hats, and sunglasses."

Mack peered in the direction Johnny had indicated. It took him a minute or so, but when he finally spotted the two men, he was sure Johnny could have been referring to no one else. There in the heart of that capacity crowd were two men he knew well. For a moment, he shook his head and wiped his eyes as though he could not believe what he was seeing. Then he looked again. They were still there: Coach Ed Smitson and Vice Principal Harold Ames.

"Wow," he said. "Holy hell, I wonder what they're doing here and what they're doing together."

Johnny smiled. "Probably here to watch a ball game."

"Yep. Let's give them a good one."

The first three innings passed quickly—no runs, no hits, no errors for either side. Johnny was having no trouble at all with the first time through the high school lineup, but neither was Louis Jones having any problems with the Yellow Jackets until the bottom of the fourth.

With Johnny pitching and a designated hitter taking a spot in the batting order, Mack had taken over the leadoff position. He was determined to get on base one way or another to give their best hitters an opportunity to bring him in. He was set for a Louis Jones—fastball. He got one, and disregarding everything he had worked on as a hitter, Mack swung about as hard as he could. He was likely as surprised as Jones when he connected solidly and sent a long fly down the left field line. It was at least twenty feet foul, but he had hit it well. *That worked out better than I expected. I really wasn't planning on hitting anything anywhere on that pitch,* he thought. Mack noted that the left side of the infield and outfield had taken a couple of steps back. *That was the plan.* He took two big practice swings and dug in. He let go a curveball away for ball one, then between pitches, tried to make it look like he really wanted to take another big swing. On the next pitch, he instead squared around and laid a decent bunt down the third baseline. The third baseman, Ostler, might have thrown him out if he had gotten to the bunt a bit sooner. As it was, Mack had the YJ's first hit, a bunt single.

He rested on the first-base bag, seemingly content, took the obligatory six-foot lead, but as Jones glanced toward him once and went into his windup, Mack kept walking, then abruptly took off for second. The catcher's throw might have been on time but was about shoulder high and Mack slid in with a stolen base. Now he was in scoring position if one of the next three batters could move him around.

Geena Daniels tried. She pushed a ground ball toward the hole between first and second, but Red made a great stop on the edge of the outfield grass and threw her out. On the throw, Mack made it easily into third with only one out. Alan Alford wasted no time. On the first pitch, he connected on a Jones fastball and sent it high and far, just not quite far enough for the hoped-for home run. Lamont Stevens hauled it in right up against the fence in deep straightaway center field. Mack scored easily for a 1–0 Yellow Jacket lead. Sam Jackson and Stan Borison grounded out to end the inning.

When the YJs took the field in the top of the fifth, the chanting started. Johnny walked the first batter while the singsong rhyme filled the air. He glanced at Mack briefly but did not give the agreed signal. The next Lion batter, Amos Jenkins, immediately doubled into the left center field gap. Ostler scored from first to tie the game. The chant level deepened, "Johnny Rainbow. Johnny Rainbow." DeQuan Ellis walked on a 3–2 pitch, runners now on first and second. Karl McKyer called a time-out and jogged out to the mound. "Johnny

Rainbow. Johnny Rainbow." It seemed like well more than half the crowd had joined the chant. Johnny assured the coach that he was okay, but on the next pitch, an inside fastball clipped Fly Waters on the hip to load the bases. Sam Jackson called another time-out and walked out to the mound. "Johnny Rainbow," the crowd chanted. Johnny did two things. He said at once to Sam, "I'm all right now." At the same time, he turned briefly in Mack's direction and gave the thumbs-up signal.

Mack raised both arms. The reserve team members on the YJ bench ran as quickly as possible out of the dugout and around the back of the infield fencing to the front of the grandstand. Johnny took a few moments to grab the resin bag and rub up the baseball. Mack dropped both arms and as one, the team in the field and along the sideline began their own staccato chant, "Johnny. Johnny. Johnny Rainbow." Clap, clap, clap over and over again. And several areas in the stands erupted with the same words in the same rhythm. "Johnny. Johnny. Johnny Rainbow." Clap, clap, clap.

By this time, the crowd was mostly on its feet and everyone seemed to be yelling one chant or the other. From his shortstop vantage point, Mack could see a core group, including Tad and Katy, and surprise, Elana yelling with the team. He saw Jana and their mom yelling as only he knew they could. And there was another section of the crowd that Mack knew to be Johnny's group of buddies. They were on their feet yelling, "Johnny. Johnny Rainbow" Clap. Clap. And he saw Ed Smitson and VP Ames on their feet with their Lincoln hats, seemingly chanting with the Yellow Jackets too. The umpire was yelling also, but best guesses had him saying, "Play ball," though no one could actually hear him. It was as much bedlam as a high school field with about two thousand spectators could manage.

Johnny, however, was smiling and waving at the crowd. And with what could only be called a particularly dramatic flair, he signaled for quiet, not unlike a politician who has something significant to say. And amazingly enough, the noise almost abruptly subsided. What emerged momentarily was scattered applause rising to a crescendo. Johnny managed a slight bow. He didn't attempt a speech. Instead, he leaned in for Sam's sign and fired a fastball over the inside corner for strike one on Trey McCarthy, the high school left fielder. He struck Trey out on three pitches, the last a sharp inward breaking slider. Most of the crowd roared its approval. Then with one out and the count 2–2, J. J. Jackson did connect with Johnny's fastball but sent a grounder slightly to Mack's left—a nearly perfect double play ball. Mack gloved it, flipped to Chen at second, and Larry threw a strike to Karl McKyer at first. Inning over.

I would be happy if we could just declare the game won now and go home, thought Mack as he jogged in from his shortstop position. But unfortunately or not, it was still only the fifth inning and the score was now tied again. After that chaotic fifth, Johnny was superb. The Lion coaches and a couple of the players did their best to rattle him but usually in the time-honored baseball chatter with only subtle jabs at his character—things like "We're going to take you out this inning, boy," or "He can't pitch," or "You throw like a girl." At which Geena took great umbrage, quickly searching her agile mind for an appropriate comeback and settling on "Careful, little boys, or I'll tell your mama." None of this appeared to affect Johnny. If anything, he looked stronger through the seventh and eighth. His fastball seemed to have an extra zip to it. His slider broke more sharply. The strikeouts began to pile up. He had nine going into the ninth inning. Some of the crowd behind the Lions dugout heard Hanson challenge his players with quiet but rather menacing words, "Come on, guys. Let's teach this sissy boy a lesson." And as the innings wore on, the rhetorical question was asked, "You gonna let this gay-wad beat you?"

Taking their cue from Johnny, the YJs pretended to be oblivious to most of the more mean-spirited chatter. They continued to support him during and between innings, "Hang in there, kid. We'll get you some runs," "All right, Johnny. You got 'em right where you want 'em," and "Can't hit 'em if they can't see 'em." And on every strikeout, "Strike three, baby," as they whipped the ball around the infield. And "Let 'em hit, Johnny. We're behind you." That was the only one they didn't really mean. The YJs were fine if no Lion bats touched a ball for the rest of the game.

Meanwhile, Jones, for the high school, was not nearly as effective as he had been in the early innings. The Yellow Jackets had runners on base every inning. They just couldn't seem to come up with a timely hit in the right situation. In the seventh, they loaded the bases on two singles and a walk with one out. Jones obviously didn't like it, but Hanson brought in Garry Matthews as a reliever and Matthews was up to the situation, striking out both Larry Chen and Jason Denard, the DH.

Randal James, the starting left fielder (with Johnny pitching, Georgeena had moved to center), struck out to open the bottom of the eighth. But Josh Kelsey, pinch hitting for Coach McKyer, drove a flare into right center field for a single, then took second when the right fielder bobbled the ball. That brought up Mack, and it also brought Hanson back out to the mound. He talked to Matthews briefly and then waved in Jason Phelps from the bullpen to face Mack with the game on the line.

While Phelps took his warm-up tosses, Mack took his time selecting his bat, rubbing the handle, putting on, then taking off his batting gloves and making several practice swings. But mostly, he was thinking—thinking about the many ups and downs of the season. Briefly, his mind touched on those last few weeks of school and his anger and grief when he didn't make the high school team, the chaos created by the aftermath of the prom fight and his strange relationship with Elana, and his hesitance to play in the commercial league on his dad's team. But mostly, he thought about Johnny, their personal practice times, his struggle to understand, and finally, to appreciate their friendship. And he thought, *This game, this is Johnny's time, Johnny's game. But it is also my game, my time. And whatever happens, I will remember this game, this time, for as long as I remember anything.*

Mack decided he wanted to feel the bat, skin on handle. He left the gloves off, rubbed the moisture off his hands, then walked slowly toward the plate. He half saw Jason Phelps's face—noticed in passing the same strange, seemingly smug, possibly intimidating, maybe arrogant grin he had seen during the high school tryouts and much more recently, last night. He noticed but quickly disregarded whatever he saw. It was just a look. Jason Phelps was just a guy. Jason

Phelps was not the enemy. He was only a guy who wanted to strike him out. For now, Jason Phelps the person didn't matter—only the ball he held in his throwing hand mattered.

At that moment, Mack was so focused on the ball, he almost forgot what he was supposed to do to it. Jason's first pitch buzzed inside, slightly under his chin. Mack barely leaned back enough to avoid getting hit. That woke him up from his semi-philosophical daze—perhaps not the reaction the pitcher was looking for. Mack had been nearly too relaxed. Now he was ready. The second pitch was Jason's slow curve, which dropped over the outside corner for a strike. For a split second, Mack considered attempting to the drive the ball toward right. He didn't swing—one and one the count. The third pitch was another inside fastball, but the umpire thought it caught the edge—one ball, two strikes.

Will he try to get me to chase outside again? No, don't over think. Focus. Stay focused on the ball. Keep your weight on your back foot. Let your hand-eye coordination go to work. Start your swing. Compact stride. Step into it. Keep your eye on the ball. Focus. Focus. The crowd noise increased. Mack ignored it. The catcher, his old football friend Amos, made some comment in an effort to distract him. Mack ignored it. Jason Phelps glanced at the runner dancing off second base, pivoted, and again fired the ball toward Mack's head. Mack's eye followed the ball. He did not duck. He saw the spin, saw it as the ball started to break and dive a few feet before it crossed the plate. He held his swing a slight split second. If it had been a fastball, it would have been by him before he could start his swing. As it was, his timing could not have been better. Swing. Crack (or *bonk* as we say in aluminum language). The ball began as a rising line drive headed to straightaway left field. This time, it did not bend left toward the foul pole but kept on flying and flying—a home run in most any league.

A quick look toward the outfield and Mack knew he did not have to run to first, but he did anyway, then tagging the bag and taking the turn, he enjoyed the trot around the bases and of course, the cheers from his teammates and from the gathered fans. Who wouldn't? *That is certainly a feeling I wouldn't mind having again*, he thought. He rounded third, received a hand slap from his dad who was coaching there, and when he hit home plate, everybody from the team was there for high fives, shoulder slaps, and even a hug or two. Yellow Jackets 3, Lions 1. Could they go home now? No, there were still three more outs to go.

If only things were that easy. And they might have been, except this was baseball and as the old Yogi Berra—quote goes, "It ain't over till it's over." Maybe there was a bit of a letdown somewhere, although a 3–1 lead is hardly enough to encourage one. In any case, the Lions were not ready to roll over and play dead yet. The top of the Lincoln order had not done much all game, but in the ninth, DeQuan Ellis led off with a bunt single. Then Fred Waters lined another base hit to straightaway center. Ellis went all the way to third. Geena tried to cut him down, but her throw was late and Waters took second. Two on in scoring position, nobody out. Mack called time and trotted to the mound to say something to Johnny, but when he got there, the look of determination on Johnny's face was such that Mack found he had nothing to say. "You got 'em" was all he took time for.

Johnny struck out Trey McCarthy again, this time on four pitches. One down, two to go. J. J. Jackson stepped in, and a ten-pitch duel commenced. Three times J. J. fouled off 3–2 pitches before finally working Johnny for a walk. The bases were loaded for Carlisle Williamson.

Mack liked Carlisle a lot. They had been good teammates on both the football and basketball teams. Carlisle was more of a football lineman than a baseball player at heart. He was a good six-four, 240 pounds of solid muscle. Standing at the plate, Carlisle looked like a hitter and someone capable of hitting the ball a long way. Mack had been somewhat puzzled by what he had noticed about Carlisle's hitting thus far and that was clearly in his mind when his friend stepped into the batter's box. Whatever the situation these past two games, Carlisle had always hit the ball straight up the middle. Mack subtly shifted a couple of feet toward second.

On a 2–2 pitch, Johnny attempted to fool Carlisle with a slow curve. Carlisle was not fooled, and he hammered the pitch straight up the middle. But Mack was on the move before Carlisle swung. As it was, he had almost waited too long. It was two long steps and then a rather diving lunge, and he came up with the ball on its second hop almost directly behind second. A backhand flip to Chen covering made for out number two. Larry tried to double up Williamson at first, but Carlisle beat the throw by a step. DeQuan Ellis scored on the play. It was now 3–2, with Lions on first and third and two outs. Lamont Stevens was the Lion hitter.

No one had to remind Johnny of how dangerous Stevens was. Mack briefly thought that an intentional walk would be a good strategy. When Mack trotted to the mound to suggest that, Johnny didn't say a word. He did shake his head. And he was careful. He teased Lamont with soft stuff, a slow curve off the corner, a changeup that Stevens was way in front of, a fastball well off the plate. The count came full. *He'll walk him or try to get him to chase another curve off the plate*, thought Mack. He moved a step or two back and toward the hole. Then Johnny, maybe on the last pitch of his short baseball career, put everything he had into a fastball, a bit low but over the heart of the plate. Lamont swung, but he didn't touch it. Strike three, game over, series tied one apiece.

CHAPTER 29

The Series: Game III

Mack liked football—especially the unified physical effort and struggle it took to forge a team's way down the field against an often equal and motivated team effort to stop you and reverse directions. And Mack liked basketball—the intricate work of five guys combining their strengths and skills in one coordinated effort to put a large round ball into a relatively small basket more often than one's opponents. Of course, they were both a whole lot more complicated than a one-sentence description.

But over the last few days, Mack began to realize that, though he may possibly like every sport ever invented—at least all those involving some kind of ball—it was baseball that he loved best. He was certainly aware that not everyone, including the three sport athletes he knew and a certain sister, shared his feelings. Finding precise words for his preference was difficult.

He loved the challenges of baseball: the confrontation between pitcher and hitter, the strategies that rarely worked exactly as planned, the possibility of something unique happening every time you played a game, the diamond layout of the field, the prep time and the waiting when nothing much is happening that suddenly becomes a flurry of critical action, the poetry of a good catch, the brief pause when a ball is launched into the air and you don't know where it will land, the sounds of the game (the crack of bat on ball, the encouraging chatter, the sellers in the stands crying out their wares—peanuts, popcorn, Cracker Jacks, hot dogs, soda, ice-cold beer, etc.), the history, the strange record setting that seems to emerge every time professional teams play, the memorabilia, and the sense that anyone of any size and shape can become a player at some level if they want to.

Finally, it was baseball that provided him with so many metaphors about how he wanted to live his life: dealing with victory and loss and his role in them; being flexible enough to change a plan or strategy when needed; knowing that—maybe a third of the time at the most—he would be successful at what he set out to accomplish; recognizing that when he had a bad day, someone else would more than likely have a good one; and so on and so on.

Mack felt—as he walked toward the mound to throw his first pitch in the third game of the series between his Yellow Jackets and his high school Lions—that somehow, he was participating in a much broader history. Not that the written or video accounts of this game would make it into the national baseball archives but that he trusted his teammates, and they trusted him, to do their best to make good memories that would last, win or lose. At the start of the season, he had not realized how much growing up he had to do (maybe one never does). He had been so focused on himself—his failures and his broken dreams—that he had been unable to focus on the here and now. He could not thank baseball and the Yellow Jackets for changing all that, but he was grateful for the role the team had played.

As he looked around the field, he felt the connection and support of every single one: his infield mates; Larry Chen, his double-play partner; Randal, at first who had scooped many of his errant throws out of the dirt; Al, who held down the hot corner with aplomb; Josh, a capable if less experienced backup at short; and the outfielders. There was Johnny, his friend, back in his accustomed spot in center, fast and sure-handed with an arm like a rocket launcher; Stan in right with a strong arm as well, who hustled to back up every play on the right side of the field; and Georgeena, who had easily proven that a woman could hold her own in this game. There were Sam behind the plate and Peter Morgan on the bench who had been two of the best pitching mentors he could have imagined. There were the other guys, those who usually started on the bench: Andrew, who had provided him with a listening ear when he most needed that; and Jason, who had never begrudged two young guys replacing most of his pitching minutes and had been their most outspoken support, especially in the Johnny Rainbow—plan.

Finally, there was Coach/Dad. When you're a kid, do you ever really know your parents? Mack's dad was not perfect. He had never claimed to be. But he was a good guy who loved his kids and wanted what was best for them. Deep down, Mack had known that, but he hadn't always appreciated it. He saw now how often he was critical and dismissive instead of interested in his dad's thoughts or opinions. He saw how anxious and impatient and even obnoxious he had been when he was sure he knew more about life than his dad. Since becoming a teenager, he really hadn't experienced or allowed himself to experience his dad as a leader. Now looking around, he could see the trust and respect that his fellow YJs showed Karl McKyer. He had experienced his dad valuing his opinion but not treating him with undue favoritism.

As he threw a few more warm-up pitches, Mack took a couple of moments to subtly glance at the crowd, which if anything was larger than the previous day. There were Jana and their mom and the group of Johnny's friends, who all—for some reason unknown to Mack—had dressed in pink and purple. There were a bunch of Mack's athlete buddies from the football and basketball teams. They would likely be rooting for the Lions or perhaps just hoping for a good game. There were also some of Mack's other high school friends, many of whom had provided significant support for the Johnny Rainbow—response. Tad and Katy were there again. When she saw him glance in their direction, Katy stood up and waved. Mack barely resisted the temptation to wave back. That would definitely rank as unacceptable in the athletic hero manual. With his resistance came a brief twinge of what Mack recognized as jealousy. What was that about? And there again—and he still had no idea what to make of it— were Coach Smitson and VP Ames that day, also joined by basketball Head Coach Michael Phillips. He resisted further exploration for the moment. There was a game to play and a few more warm-up pitches to throw. *Focus, Mack, focus.*

He had begun this baseball season with revenge as his strongest motivation, revenge and the need to prove himself. Now he still wanted to win. But he wanted to do so for his team, for the guys (and gal) who had taken him in and been patient with his stupidity, his wounds, and his wounded pride. He looked around one more time and thought about yelling, "This is for you," to all of them, but likely, no one would have understood, so he only allowed himself the gesture of throwing up his pitching hand in a half salute half wave. Then he turned to the task at hand.

"Now the starting batteries for today's game. Catching, Sam Jackson. And pitching for the Columbia City Sporting Goods Yellow Jackets, Francis 'Mack' McKyer." Was it Mack's imagination or did a sizable portion of the crowd rise from a murmur to a definite stir with that announcement? Were they saying things like, "McKyer— why isn't he playing for the high school team?" But his inner dialogue quickly shifted back to this moment he had been thinking about for the last two months.

The first batter in Hanson's renovated lineup for game three was Kerry "Red" Fergeson, Mack's best friend. Now was not a time for best friend sentiment. Red managed a ground ball foul off Mack's fastball, then struck out on a change.

Next up, Fly Waters stepped in, grinned at Mack, and yelled, "Throw it where I can see it."

Mack yelled back, "It's not a football, Fly. It's small, white, and round."

The Fly, however, did not see it that clearly. He struck out swinging on a fastball just above his knees and walked away shaking his head. J. J. Jackson, also friend and football running back, was not as talkative. With a nearly .400 batting average and fifteen home runs, he also had proven to be one of the better hitters in the city league for the season. He, as the saying goes, "let his bat do his talking for him." J. J. got a fairly decent piece of the ball but grounded it directly to Josh at short. Mack took an anxious deep breath, but Josh handled the ball cleanly and threw out J. J. easily. Three up, three down.

The high school starting pitcher was a guy the YJs had not seen before—Trevor Samielson. Like Levinsky, Trevor threw from the left side but more like Louis Jones, Samielson was fast. He was also a little on the wild side. Johnny Raymond walked on four pitches to start the YJ half of the first. On the second pitch, Geena bunted, sending Johnny to second. Samielson fielded the ball and threw out Geena by a couple of strides. Al Alford swung on the first pitch and sent a towering fly to deep left field for the second out. Johnny died on second when Sam Jackson struck out on a 3–2 curveball about a foot outside.

Mack continued to throw effectively through the fourth inning. Five of the twelve outs were strikeouts, four were routine infield ground balls, and two were pop flies easily gathered in by Chen at second and Geena Daniels in short left field. The only scary moment for Mack was Trey McCarthy's long fly ball, which Johnny ran down in deep right center in the third.

Trevor Samielson was nearly as good. Since the first, he had scattered singles by Chen, Borison, and Raymond. Johnny stole second but got no further in the bottom of the third. Samielson walked two and hit one—Sam Jackson—in the fourth. But he also struck out six and was helped out by two double plays. So far, it was a classic pitcher's duel, not unlike the day before.

Things changed dramatically in the fifth, and it all happened with two outs. Johnny punched a line drive just inside the right field foul line and coasted into second with a double. Samielson then walked both Daniels and Alford to load the bases. Sam Jackson came up with the whole YJ dugout and half the crowd screaming for a hit. He delivered with a drive into the right center field gap. The runners were off at the crack of the bat. Johnny and Geena scored easily. The center fielder, Lamont Stevens finally picked up the ball, which had ricocheted off the wall toward deep center. He turned and fired a strike to the cutoff man, Kerry Fergeson, who threw his own strike to the catcher. Alford, lumbering around third like an aging express train, was not about to stop and barreled into the Lions catcher Jenkins. Amos was a burly tight end on the football team and was not about to let Alford run over him. It was a case of train meeting immovable wall. The wall won, and Jenkins held on to the ball for the third out of the inning. But now, the YJs led 2–0.

Flash forward three more innings. The score remained the same, and Mack had yet to give up a single hit. For the first time in his pitching career—such as it was—he was in a groove, oblivious to anything that would distract him from getting and agreeing to his catcher's signs, gripping the ball in his glove, winding up and eyeing his target at the same time, firing each of his pitches with the same ease and motion. Three up, three down. Three up, three down. Top of the ninth. The score was now 3–0 after another double by Johnny followed by an RBI single from Geena Daniels in the bottom of the eighth.

The Lions were desperate and determined. Coaches Hanson and Ramsey were both striding back and forth, trying to rally their team. The crowd murmur gradually increased as the high school fans implored their team to rally and the first high school hitter stepped up to the plate. For the first time in the game, Mack felt tired. His first two pitches to the Lion pinch hitter, Jerry Corbett, were high and well out of the strike zone. An anxious Corbett swung at the second one anyway and missed it for strike one. Mack overcompensated and threw the next two pitches low. On the 3–1 count, Mack was determined not to walk Corbett and grooved the pitch right down the middle. Corbett swung and grounded sharply toward short. Josh Kelsey gloved the ball okay but hurried his throw to first. It was well over Randal's head, and before he could recover the ball, Jerry Corbett stood on second base.

Hopeful high school fans began a rhythmic clap. Another pinch hitter stepped in—Ryan Ostler. Ryan had suffered a serious injury during the football season. Mack had visited him in the hospital several times and a new friendship had blossomed. Ryan had fully recovered well in time for the baseball season and had become the Lions starting third baseman for most of the season. As he took his practice swings, Ostler looked confident. A brief mound visit from Sam Jackson helped restore Mack's focus. He pitched carefully to Ryan—too carefully—and walked him on a full count with a fastball the umpire ruled a wee bit outside. Mack managed to control a shake of his head in disagreement. No time for that.

Two on, one out, and up stepped his good friend Kerry again. Friend or not, Mack was determined to throw the ball by him. Red seemed to sense this and did his best to wait Mack out. Two off-speed pitches missed the outside corner. Red fouled off the first fastball. And the next one Mack threw was in the dirt, a wild pitch, and both runners advanced. Mack's slider caught the plate for strike two, but on the 3–2 count, Red connected with enough of Mack's fastball to send a high fly ball to left. Georgeena made the catch, but Jerry Corbett scored the high school's first run. There was now one out, but to Mack, the inning and the game felt like they were slipping away—without a hit.

With Ostler still on second, Fly Waters stepped in, on orders from his coach to make sure he looked things over. Fly had a good eye and didn't lift the bat off his shoulder until yet another full count. He swung late on Mack's 3–2 fastball and drove the ball on the ground to Larry Chen's left. Chen had been the most reliable YJ infielder all season, but though he had plenty of time and space to glove the Waters grounder, Larry booted it. Before he could recover the ball in short right field, Ostler was on third and the Fly made it all the way to second when Josh Kelsey forgot to cover the bag. Runners were again on second and third with still only one down.

The YJ infield, catcher, and coach gathered with Mack on the mound. Both Larry and Josh were quick in blaming themselves for the current jam. Frankly, Mack would have liked to blame them too. But he took some of it on, simply saying, "This is on me. I haven't been that sharp this inning." It was Sam and then coach/Dad who settled them down.

"Okay," said Sam, "there's plenty of blame to go around. I've got some, too, letting that one pitch get by me. But blaming is not going to get us through the next two outs."

"I couldn't agree more," said Karl McKyer. "Let's all focus on now. How tired are you, Mack? Softy is ready to come in if we need him."

"Check with Sam, but I think I'm strong enough to finish." To which Sam added, "Seems to me he's still got it, boss, as long as he doesn't think he has to do it by himself."

"Did you hear that, Mack?" Mack nodded. "Then we're set. All of you—all of you forget the last few plays. We're still ahead. I'd rather be us than them. Focus. Think through and know what you'll do if the ball comes to you. Throw strikes, Mack! This is our game to lose. And if we do, so what? It's just a game. Have fun. I will not cancel the end-of-season picnic no matter what."

That broke up the meeting with a laugh just as the umpire stepped out to remind everyone to—are you ready for it—"Play ball."

So Ostler on third, Waters on second, one out, and J. J. Jackson (the number three hitter) coming to the plate. On the first pitch, Jackson obviously wanted to end the game with a big fly. He swung and missed Mack's changeup by about a foot and nearly fell to his knees. There was a collective "Ah," from the crowd. Mack's second pitch was a slider over the outside corner for strike two. J. J. glanced at the umpire as if to say, "You've got to be kidding me." Mack's intention was to tease Jackson with an outside curveball, but J. J. guessed another changeup and swung over the pitch for the third strike. Two outs now, but the tying runs still in scoring positions.

Carlisle Williamson was the hitter. Mack thought about walking him to load the bases, but that would bring up Lamont Stevens and Mack decided he would rather pitch to Carlisle. Before putting a foot on the pitching rubber, he again looked around the field at his teammates. *Would Carlisle continue his hitting pattern?* Mack spent an extra second staring out at Johnny Raymond in center. He wasn't sure, but it looked like Johnny saluted him. *I hope I know what that means,* he thought. Then Mack turned to face the hitter.

Carlisle took a first-pitch strike on a slider, then watched a slow curve bend just off the plate. On the 1–1 count, he leveled off on Mack's fastball and drove it on a line straight over Mack's head and second base toward center field. As Mack watched, he saw both runners off and running. They would score easily. He saw the game and the series disappearing. He ran to back up Sam Jackson in case there was a throw toward the plate. Mack's back was turned, so he missed Johnny's sprint from deep center. He heard the crowd gasp, but he didn't see Johnny leaning forward and reaching out his glove at the last possible moment. He did turn in time to see Johnny's head over heels somersault and bounce to his feet. He saw Johnny reach into his glove, reach in, and pull out a baseball. He looked quickly toward the infield umpire whose fist was raised in the air.

For a brief moment, it was as though all the air collapsed out of his body and he realized he had been holding his breath for far too long. The game was over. The YJs had won 3–1. And as unlikely as it seemed, he had actually pitched a no-hitter. Then came the team in from the field and from the dugout and even some folks from the grandstand. And they all were whooping and hollering as though they had captured the World Series instead of the best two out of three in a playoff game between Lincoln High School and the Columbia City Sporting Goods Yellow Jackets of the Columbia City commercial league. It was a great moment for the YJs nonetheless. And here came Johnny "Rainbow" Raymond, still running full out with the game ball in his hand. Mack braced himself, and it was a good thing because Johnny leaped and Mack caught him, a full-body hug between two friends, two guys who both loved baseball. For the moment, Mack didn't even think about being embarrassed.

A few minutes later, after receiving congratulations from a lot of people—some of whom he knew and others not—Mack sat in the dugout, replaying the game and shaking his head in disbelief. They had done it—he and Johnny and their YJ crew of misfits. What a game! What a season! Now what? Then it hit him. Preseason football practice would start in three weeks.

EPILOGUE

Two Mid-Season Conversations
(The first at a local coffee house sometime in June)

Johnny: You go to church, right?

Mack: Sometimes—not as often as the rest of my family but yeah.

Johnny: So you consider yourself a Christian.

Mack: Yeah, I guess. I haven't really thought about it. What about you?

Johnny: Not really. My parents aren't really religious, but when I was younger, my granny took me to church with her. She was as Christian as they come. It was okay for a while. I mean, people were friendly enough and I liked the music part. It was the Bible study stuff, and when I was about twelve, I really started listening to the Bible studies and the sermons.

Mack: Whatdya mean?"

Abruptly, Johnny stood up and pulled over a music stand that was set in the corner of the nearly empty coffeehouse space and placed it in front of him. He cleared his throat, then said in a raspy, unnatural sounding voice that obviously was an imitation of a preacher he had once heard, "Leviticus 20:13 says, 'If a man also lie with mankind as he lieth with a woman, both of them have committed an abomination: they shall surely be put to death, that there be no wickedness among you.' Or how about this one from the New Testament. Romans 1:26–27, 31, says, 'For this cause God gave them up unto vile affections: for even their women did change the natural use into that which is against nature: And likewise also the men leaving the natural use of the woman, burned in their lust one toward another; men with men, working that which is unseemly… Knowing the judgment of God that they that commit such things are worthy of death.'" He sat down. "So that's what I mean."

Mack: Wow, well, that's pretty distressing. I don't think I've ever heard those read. Why on earth or why in hell did you memorize them?

Johnny: Hey, it's the Bible, the Christian's sacred book, right? Your sacred book. Anyway, in the Sunday school Granny took us to, we got extra M&M cookies from Ms. Charlotte if we memorized the verses she assigned. And maybe you can guess why she assigned those to me, although I didn't much think about it at the time. I just wanted the cookies.

Mack: But I don't know. I don't know the Bible that well, but I think that stuff you had to learn—I know for the cookies—isn't that important or central to the main message.

Johnny: And what would that be?

Mack: I, uh, maybe something like we're supposed to love each other. Something like that.

Johnny: Fair enough. I could be for that. But the story from this boy is that the church teaches that people like me aren't welcome there.

Mack: Johnny, I don't think I have a lot riding on whether you are a Christian or not. That's up to you, but if you're going to reject something—something significant anyway—then I think maybe you should decide that based on what people actually believe and how they treat you rather than one boyhood set of experiences with a church.

Johnny: That's fine for you to say. When you go to church, you don't have to look around the place wondering who there is judging you because the Bible says you are a sinner worthy of death or who definitely wouldn't want you in their church if they knew who and what you were.

Mack: You're right. If I felt like that, I wouldn't want to go to church either.

Their discussion didn't stop there. As for Johnny, he hadn't expected to change his mind and decide to go back to church, though he did ask himself why he had brought up the whole matter in the first place. He had expected Mack to get defensive like other churchgoing friends and acquaintances usually did. When Mack had basically agreed with him, he was more or less at a loss. Was Mack that different or did different churches teach different things? That seemed kind of weird. Didn't they all believe the same Bible?

Mack was a bit more upset than he let on. And he didn't know what, if anything, to do about it. He had felt like he somehow needed to defend Christianity, even though he wasn't all that involved in church himself. *What was that about?* He thought about his parents' church, which maybe was his, too, or as close as he came to one. What did their church teach about LGBTQ issues? He had no idea. He had never really thought about it before. That had nothing to do with him or did it?

At the next YJ practice, Mack was in the dugout sitting next to Pepper Wexler. Both of them were waiting for their turn at the plate when Mack was suddenly struck by a thought. He acted on it before he could chicken out.

"Hey, Pepper, didn't my dad tell me you were some kind of minister?"

Pepper stared at him blankly. "You mean that rumor's going around again—must be the halo over my head."

It was Mack's turn to stare blankly. "Uh." Pepper laughed.

"Mack, Mack, I was just kidding. Yes, I confess, I'm a minister, pastor, clergyman—whatever you prefer. Who wants to know?"

"Well, me, I do. I wonder if I could talk to you sometime, you know, professionally or whatever it's called."

"Sure. When would work for you? I keep office hours, usually from one through five at my church or I could meet you at the Spoon or someplace like that.

"No, no, definitely not the Spoon. Your office would be fine. And please don't tell my dad."

They worked out the details, agreeing to a three-o'clock appointment the following Thursday.

*****

Mack had timed things so that he could get to work at four. He figured about a half hour was all the time he would need. He parked his mom's car three blocks away from the church building and down a side street. He realized—as he walked toward the church building—that if it were not summer and nearly 80 degrees, he would probably have hidden under some clothing disguise. As it was, he pulled his Chicago Cubs hat down as far as it would go, stayed in tree shadows as much as possible, and glanced away whenever any traffic went by. *What if someone recognizes me?*

He hurried his pace as he approached the front door. What was he so intimidated about? Pepper—*Rev. Wexler* he self-corrected—was a nice guy. And a Presbyterian Church was hardly some kind of weird cult. Nevertheless, Mack was nervous. *What if he laughs at me or doesn't take me seriously or thinks I'm ignorant and stupid?* It didn't help when Mack, hoping to slip quickly inside, tried the large churchy looking doors in front and discovered they were locked. *Of course, they're locked, stupid. It's not Sunday morning.* He looked quickly around and nearly jumped a foot off the ground when a car driving by honked sharply before turning the corner. *Okay, that does it. I'm not meant to keep this appointment,* which was ridiculous, of course.

About then, he noticed the signed directions beside the door with offices and an arrow pointing toward the side of the building. He followed the arrow and made his way through a glassed door to a reception area. There was no one there, but again on the wall, there were signs: "This way to the counseling center. This way to—" Wait a second. He wasn't here to go to any counseling center. Is that what Pepper thought? *Oh great, I wonder if you have to pay for that. I did say I wanted his professional help, or did I?* Before he could take that thought through to any conclusion, there was Rev. Pepper Wexler emerging from the counseling center area. He waved at Mack, thanked him for being on time, and then shepherded him the other direction. Again, there was a sign, this time directed to anyone who cared to look toward the pastor's office. Pepper waved for Mack to enter the space ahead of him.

It was not a huge office by any means, but it was comfortable appearing. A large desk sat in one corner near a window looking out toward a parklike setting. The walls were lined with bookshelves, except for a couple of spaces for some spiritually themed artwork. There was a seating area out in front of the desk—large enough for two chairs, a small sofa, and a coffee table.

"Have a seat, Mack. Can I get you anything to drink—tea, soda, water?"

"No, thanks." Mack sat on one of the chairs, and Pepper Wexler took the other one.

"So what's on your mind?"

I might as well get right to it, he thought. "I want to know what your church teaches about homosexuality. And before you say anything, this is not about me. I mean it is in one way but not because I'm questioning my own orientation. I'm good. I mean I'm heterosexual. I'm not gay." Even to himself, Mack was thinking, *I do protest too much. Why am I making this so awkward?*

"Before we go any further, you said at practice that you didn't want me to tell your dad. I'm reassuring you that whatever you have to say is just between you and me. The only time I would break that promise is if I thought you were of potential harm to yourself or someone else, okay?"

"Okay, I guess. I thought so but thanks. I'll try to be more coherent going forward. I really don't know why I'm nervous about this. It is about my friend who is gay. We were talking the other day, and well, he grew up in this church—his granny's church actually—and definitely felt unwelcome there. But he kept going because she wanted him to and he didn't really think he had a choice. And it's like he was pretty involved as a kid and even memorized verses from the Bible because, well, because that's what they did and he wanted to be like everyone else, I guess. Anyway, he actually quoted a couple of those verses to me. And he said he didn't believe in Christianity anymore and he didn't know why he still remembered those verses and why he was telling all of this to me. But anyways, it made me think and I'm not sure what I believe either. I guess I had never really thought about any of this before. I mean I didn't want to get in an argument with him, but then again, I'm not sure he's wrong to have left the church. But then again, I didn't want to misrepresent what Christians believe, even when I'm not sure I am one."

Mack paused for a breath. He felt like he was overtalking the whole thing. *Why am I here? Do I care that much about some obscure verses from the Bible?*

As if he was reading Mack's mind, Pepper Wexler asked, "Why are you here, Mack?" Mack sighed.

"I'm not really sure. I'm just confused. I thought I kind of knew what I believed. No, it's not that. What it is, Pepper, is I could tell that even after however many years have gone by, my friend is still hurting from whatever happened in that church. In some ways, they taught him to hate who he is. If this is what the church teaches or at best ignores, then I don't want any part of it either. There is too much hate in the world and I don't want to be part of it, but I don't know what to do about it either. So you can help me, just a little maybe, by telling me what the church believes about gay people."

"That may be a taller order than you know. But before going any further down that road, I will state as clearly as I can that I do not personally believe that God's love is limited to straight people. I believe that God loves everything in the world, every person in the world, and that it is therefore the business of all those who are believers to love our fellow beings. Is that a clear place to start from?"

Mack nodded.

"This church—meaning the people who gather here and who support this particular institution—have taken a stand to be an open and affirming community. Do you know what that means?"

Make shook his head as he said, "No."

"It means that in our time and culture, we are willing to welcome as members and to advocate on behalf of people in the LGBTQ community. We believe this is important for some of the reasons we have been talking about, namely that people of minority sexual orientations have been abused, oppressed, and often made to feel unwelcome in the church. We have been working, with mixed success, to change those kinds of attitudes for the last forty through fifty years. Your parents attend the Disciples church over on Jefferson Street, right?" Mack nodded. "I know Rev. Carpenter there and you may not have heard anything on these issues when you have attended, but I know that they also are what we call an open and affirming congregation.

"But now, directly to your point, there is no one universal church teaching on sexual orientation. Different churches believe and teach different things. Do you remember what verses your friend had memorized?"

"I know one was from the Old Testament in one of the early books I think, and the other was from the New Testament, like maybe, oh, I'm not sure."

At that, Pepper reached for a copy of the Bible and thumbed through it for a couple of moments before reading from Leviticus 20:13, then turned quickly and read the words from Book of Romans 1:26–27. "Does any of that sound familiar?"

"They sound a little different but that's them. How did you know?"

"I'm no magician, Mack. Those are two of the seven passages in all the Bible that are named as God's supposed teaching regarding sexual orientation. Gay people refer to them as the clobber scriptures because they have been used against them. There are two main difficulties with using scripture this way. The first resides in the nature of Scripture itself. What do you know about the Bible?"

"Um, I guess, well, isn't it supposed to be the Word of God?"

"Yes and no. Now is hardly the time, even if you were interested, to give you a lesson on what most scholars teach about what the Bible is and how it came to be. And even if there was, you would end up concluding that there were lots of differing opinions. I'll tell you again what I believe. And that is that the Bible contains many books of several different types: history, poetry, theology, laws, and literature to name most of them. And some contain or express what almost all Christians would call the Word of God, but a lot of what's in the Bible reflects the culture and times when it was written. Further, even if we could agree about what the important teachings of the Bible are, there would still be major differences in interpretation. You following me thus far?"

"I think so, though I'm not making the connection to how any of this matters with respect to what the Bible says about LGBTQ folks."

"Fair enough. And it's not that simple. I'm going to give you some reading material to take home if you are interested, but what I will say in general is that to one degree or another, the Bible's teaching regarding gays, etc., reflects the cultural standards of the times and places where the writers and teachers lived. Simply put, the understanding of those ancient writers like the priestly author of Leviticus several hundred years before Christ and that of Paul's letter to the Romans were either wrong, inaccurately translated, or reflected only a limited understanding of human sexuality. Further, if—like the pastor of your friend's granny—you believe that every word of the Bible is inspired directly by God, then there are still good arguments that the meaning of the teachings in Leviticus, Genesis where we find the story of Sodom and Gomorrah, 1 Corinthians, Timothy, Thessalonians, and Romans have very little, if anything, to do with the sexual behavior of people practicing or living in faithful, loving relationships."

"But what did Jesus himself have to say?"

"Good question." And Pepper paused as though there were so many possibilities, he couldn't possibly name them all. "Nothing."

"Nothing?"

"Nothing, nada, not one thing. Not anything that we can know from the New Testament. He had a lot to say about how we treat the poor and how we treat each other and about how good we are at saying good things and not doing them. But he had nothing that we know of to say about the behavior of sexual minorities.

"To bring this back to where we started, many, many but not all Christians and churches have studied and reflected on the relationship of the Christian faith to sexual orientation and have concluded that what is important is learning to live in loving relationships, not judging others who have made different choices than ours about who and how they will love. Maybe that's a lot more info than you bargained for when you made our appointment, but I'd be glad to talk further anytime. And if you want, I'd be happy to sit down with your friend sometime as well."

*****

Like Pepper's responses to Mack's questions, I believe that their conversation is faithful to many—though certainly not all—current church understandings of the relationship between the church and the LGTBQ community. And like Rev. Pepper, I would encourage people who have further questions or interests regarding the inclusion of LGTBQ persons in the life of any religious-oriented community to seek out those communities who advertise their openness to and welcome of all people of differing sexual orientations. Approach such conversations with an open mind and a genuine interest in learning what it means to love faithfully, and I suspect your life will be enriched if not greatly changed.

ACKNOWLEDGMENTS

Appreciation is expressed to Dan, Anne, Peggy, Gerry, Allen, Laura, Janet, Mary, Bruce, Gary, John, Steve, and the many other gay, lesbian, and bisexual persons who have graced my life from time to time. Collectively, they have taught me much about justice, compassion, acceptance, courage, and grace. Some have also taught me that intolerance, shallowness, prejudice, dishonesty, and meanness are not solely heterosexual qualities. In short, they have affirmed what most of us might expect—that, indeed, we (gay and straight) are all human beings with our own unique mixes of strengths and frailties.

I especially thank my friend (and former student) Joe, who falls decidedly under the first collective grouping above and who agreed to read and provide critique for a baseball-themed book that introduced an openly gay young man as a primary character. His input was gracious, kind, and incorporated into my writing. I also add here my thanks to my youngest daughter, Kaylen, who read the preliminary script of this book and offered the invaluable perspective of the younger generation and, on occasion, prevented me from making some of the youth culture-related errors I was prone to. In turn, I taught her greater appreciation for the game of baseball—or so is my hope.

ABOUT THE AUTHOR

K. Arthur is the author of the *Seasons* series of sports-themed novels. Three of them have been completed. Four are in various planning stages. K. Arthur grew up in Seattle, Washington, where he played varsity sports in high school and at two small NAIA-affiliated colleges. He is a graduate of Milligan College (BA) and Vanderbilt University (MDiv). K. has also lived and worked in a variety of other places, including Oregon, Nova Scotia, Indiana, Colorado, Missouri, and Kentucky. Vocationally, he has been and is predominantly a professional educator, chaplain, minister, and writer. On a volunteer level, he has been both a basketball and baseball coach. K. is married and the father of four children all of whom have now survived their teen years. In the writing of *Seasons*, K. draws extensively from his experience as an athlete, coach, and parent. He currently lives with his wife and one son in Lexington, Kentucky.